GET REAL ...

LIVING EVERY DAY AS AN AUTHENTIC

FOLLOWER OF CHRIST

BRIAN JOHNSTON

Copyright © 2018 HAYES PRESS. All rights reserved. No part of this book may be reproduced, stored in a retrieval system, or transmitted in any form, without the written permission of Hayes Press.

Published by:

HAYES PRESS CHRISTIAN RESOURCES

The Barn, Flaxlands

Royal Wootton Bassett

Swindon, SN4 8DY

United Kingdom

www.hayespress.org

e: info@hayespress.org

www.facebook.com/hayespress.org

http://twitter.com/#!/hayespress

Unless otherwise indicated, all Scripture quotations are from the The Holy Bible, English Standard Version® (ESV®) Copyright © 2001 by Crossway, a publishing ministry of Good News Publishers. All rights reserved. Scriptures marked NASB are from the New American Standard Bible® (NASB®), Copyright © 1960, 1962, 1963, 1968, 1971, 1972, 1973, 1975, 1977, 1995 by The Lockman Foundation. Used by permission (www.Lockman.org). Scriptures marked RV are from the Revised Version Bible, 1885 (Public Domain). Scriptures marked KJV are from the King James Version, 1611

(Public Domain). Scriptures marked NKJV are from the HOLY BIBLE, the New King James Version® (NKJV®). Copyright © 1982 Thomas Nelson, Inc. Used by permission. All rights reserved. Scriptures marked NIV are from the New International Version®, NIV® Copyright © 1973, 1978, 1984, 2011 by Biblica, Inc.™ Used by permission. All rights reserved worldwide.

Cover image © Can Stock Photo / Nevenova

CHAPTER ONE: REALLY ACCESSING THE BIBLE'S REAL MEANING

I suppose it's fair to start by asking 'what's the basic source of information available to us as followers of Christ?' Well, that would have to be the Bible, of course. Ah, but how do we go about accessing the Bible's true meaning for our lives? That's the kind of help I could have used very early in my life as a young Christian. I wish someone had encouraged me to read the Bible as you would read any other book - and not as a mysterious text you somehow had to decode using a very specialized skill set.

What added to my struggles was the fact that I listened to preachers who attempted to explain the Bible by saying things like 'this represents that' and so on. The basis for this sort of decoding was based on what seemed to be random word associations and sometimes what I confess I took to be rather fanciful notions. A classic historical example of this type of thing comes from a story Jesus told known as the Parable of the Good Samaritan. This, as you doubtless know, concerned a man who had been mugged on a journey. None of his countrymen came to his assistance, but a foreigner did, using his donkey to transport the man to an inn. Now, in religious history, Augustine suggested the foreigner symbolized Jesus, and the donkey represented the Holy Spirit, as they came to the assistance of the human race. This is an arbitrary spiritual meaning that displaces the actual plain meaning of the words themselves. It treats the plain story as some kind of coded message: one you need to be spiritually tuned in to decode it. Be reassured, Augustine's meaning was certainly not the meaning the Lord intended to convey to his audience.

Let me clarify what I've just said – the part about reading the Bible as you would read any other book. Do I mean to say that the Bible isn't special? Of course not. I believe it to be a one of a kind book. It's unique among all books. I hold it to be God's communication to us. For sure, God accommodated himself to human language and employed human authors. But what I mean is this. Since he used humans and our language, we shouldn't expect the Bible's words to carry something other than their normal plain meanings – at least not unless the Bible itself makes it clear this is to be expected due to the type of literature being employed. An example would be when there's a clear switch from the standard narrative form to, say, a poetic form. No-one should be confused, I hope, if I say the book of Chronicles and the book of Psalms are two different kinds of literature, and we'll naturally find ourselves reading them differently.

Certainly, when we're reading the story parts of the Bible, or the letters it contains, we should look for the plain meanings carried by the words in their normal everyday use. And, of course, they follow the ordinary rules of grammar we ourselves follow in everyday communications, usually without even thinking about it.

GET REAL ... LIVING EVERY DAY AS AN AUTHENTIC FOLLOWER OF CHRIST

Another early source of confusion for me came about because I attended 'Bible studies' which consisted of debates about the Bible text where various contributors offered different reconstructions of the particular Bible section in question. Contributors would argue that the dictionary gave one meaning for a particular word of interest, whereas another contributor disagreed by pointing out the same word could have another legitimate meaning. That's when I first learnt the power of context. A particular word can indeed have a variety of meanings, but its use in a specific setting will normally determine the choice of meaning. Endless debates could have been short-circuited by simply paying more attention to the context than to the dictionary.

It can become even more misleading when it's suggested to us how Bible word meanings in the original language developed over time from more ancient 'root' or primitive forms. While this can occasionally be enlightening, it can more often be spurious. Many modern English words have come to us from their roots in the old Latin language, used by the Romans. It's easy to check that it doesn't always follow that the sense of any word as it's understood today should be influenced by a trace back to its old Latin root word.

So, what are we saying? Simply this: we should read our Bible as we would read any book. The important thing is to be observant. To emphasize the method of understanding a verse by thinking carefully about the verses that come before and after it, we can develop the habit of reading in complete paragraphs or more, and repeatedly reading that larger block of text over and over again until we catch the train of thought.

Memorising verses in isolation can all too easily mislead us when it comes to applying them in our experience. A classic example must surely be Jeremiah 29:11 from where we hear it quoted: 'I know the plans I have for you says the Lord, plans to prosper you and not to harm you, plans to give you a future and a hope.' Sounds totally reassuring, doesn't it? But this conveniently forgets the historical context of how the words were originally spoken to a disobedient people who were about to be carried away into captivity and judged, long before their descendants would in time – by virtue of this promise – return to resume their normal service. Perhaps we need to be memorising entire paragraphs rather than limited verses, or at least we need to make ourselves aware of the context of the verse we can all too glibly quote.

What we're saying is that it's an excellent habit when reading the Bible to ask basic questions of the text:

'To whom was this written?'

'And in what specific circumstances?'

'How does their reaction at the time show what they understood the message to be back then?'

That last point leads us to what some refer to as 'the golden rule' for working out what a Bible verse means to us today. It's simply this: we shouldn't expect a Bible verse to have a meaning for us that denies whatever it meant to those to whom it was first spoken. To abbreviate that: a verse cannot mean what it never meant (not unless the Bible itself later gives us a fuller expansion).

Let's repeat: meaning is determined by its (literary) context, and words are defined by their contemporary use at the time of writing. Rather than relying on historical searches after older meanings of basic forms of the same word, it's far more likely to be profitable to perform a study of how the word in question was being used by the same Bible author elsewhere in the Bible, or throughout the entire Old or New Testament, and even in literature of that same time, but outside of the Bible. Mostly, the Holy Spirit used words in the way they were generally used at the time, although it's important to recognize that some important words describe Bible ideas that require us to familiarize ourselves with how the same idea was introduced earlier in the Old Testament part of the Bible.

The safe approach is to compare all other texts related to the one we're reading. For example, the Lord did say on one occasion, 'Whatever you ask …in My name He may give to you' (John 15:16 NASB). However, when we relate this to other teachings about prayer, we find there are indeed conditions that are meant to be understood – they are taken as read in that instance and involved implicitly in what it truly means to ask in our Lord's name.

Another key idea to keep in mind when reading the Bible is to relate the topic we're considering to the mainline truths of the Bible. Sometimes, we will come across a difficult verse. Perhaps it appears at first sight to contradict other plain teaching verses. What do we do? Rather than give up in despair, we need to make the decision to always understand obscure verses in the light of verses whose meaning is clear. For example, a verse in the letter to the Hebrews has caused a lot of distress. It mentions the possibility of 'falling away' (Hebrews 6:6). But before we jump to the wrong conclusion that our forgiveness can be revoked by a God who will fail to deliver what he promised, we must realize there are two complementary mainline truths presented side by side in the Bible, namely salvation from future judgement and our service for the Lord in the here and now. God's sovereign grace guarantees our salvation, but we can fail to live up to our obligated responsibilities in serving the Lord and as a result lose some of their associated privileges in this life.

It's worth saying that we live in an age where truth has become devalued. Absolute truth is denied. What's true for you may be irreconcilably different from what's true for me, or so some say. That position, however, amounts to a denial of the God of truth and of God's Word of truth, the Bible. It leads some to say that there are many possible interpretations of any single Bible verse. "Take your pick", "Whatever works for you", they tell us. This is definitely not the way to understand the Bible. There is one correct way to interpret every single Bible verse – even if we at times struggle to grasp it. Do we think God is incapable of expressing himself clearly? No, our Lord explained certain Bible verses as critically depending on a word being singular rather than plural, and in another case the true meaning depended on the exact tense of the verb. Such precision falsifies the idea that what was conveyed was flexible enough to bear practically any meaning we might choose for it.

How then can we be sure we've found the correct meaning of any disputed text? The answer to that expands on the idea of context that we were talking about earlier. I remember a Christmas-time when my daughter was small. One of her presents was a jigsaw puzzle. In other words, a puzzle comprised of many pieces of a picture, all of them cut into different shapes. When correctly assembled, together they formed a coherent picture – in this case it was a picture of a black Labrador dog. The problem was I had thrown away the packaging which contained the only reference picture of the dog - which picture we needed to follow as our guide! This made the puzzle more challenging than it should have been. Verses of the Bible can be compared to those puzzle pieces. But when through cover-to-cover reading, we build up a sense of where the bigger picture, the meta-narrative of the Bible, is headed, we then have that as our guiding picture for how we get the unique meaning of the individual verses, including the difficult or obscure ones.

Finally, remember that it's useful to read the place we're studying from in different translations. Occasionally, this will enable us to see that sometimes there are slight differences between the original language sources available to us today, and from which all modern language versions are translated. These differences, although many, are very slight – often simply different spellings of names – and we can readily verify that no particular teaching is made in any way ambiguous by them. Just being aware of this, however, can help us to understand some slight variations in the readings.

The other useful thing about using more than one modern version is to appreciate that some translations try to get as near as possible to a word-for-word translation between the languages involved; while others translate at the level of conveying the thought behind the words. While this involves more interpretation on the part of the translators, we need to remember that any translated version will involve some element of interpretation. On these points, the notes in the margin of a study Bible will give us helpful clarification.

What we can be truly thankful to God for is the fact that we have, as a result of some detailed detective work by Bible experts, a reliably authentic representation of God's Word available to us today. It has provably the best claim in all of ancient literature to being accurate in its present form. Careful use of translations, commentaries and dictionaries, remembering the earlier points, ensures we can understand God's message for us. Most important of all, is to realize the Holy Spirit is our personal guide to help us understand it, and we can access his help by prayer ... about which we hope to have something to say in the next chapter!

CHAPTER TWO: REALLY KNOWING WHAT TO PRAY

Suppose I was to ask you, 'What's your greatest need right now?' – what would you say? Of course, that'll depend on your circumstances right now. If you should be in a small church group struggling to maintain a vibrant testimony amid a trickle of losses as other disciples give up, you might well say to me, 'Our greatest need is to reverse the ebb tide of those leaving the local church.' Or, more positively, you could say: 'Our need is to attract others by the quality of our lives of integrity.' These answers, in the situations assumed, are perfectly understandable, if not fully justified. Others among you, facing up to the protracted, debilitating illness of a loved one for whom you're caring, might say, 'Our greatest need is for a cure for this illness, so we can return to serving God as we did before.' No-one, of course, would criticize you for that. That's totally understandable. Some, experiencing God's blessings, might feel that what they need is his guiding wisdom in the responsible stewardship of the blessings they're enjoying.

Whatever your situation, I'd like to ask you to consider if there could be an even deeper need. On further reflection, might we agree that our deepest need is to know God better and have a greater sense of God in our lives? This reminds me of how we read concerning Moses (Exodus 33:18). After interceding very passionately to know better God's plans for his leading of his people, Moses concluded his intercession with the ultimate request: "Show me Your glory." That's got to be the last word in prayer request, hasn't it?

Jim Packer, and doubtless others, have written that prayer is the measure of a person. If we're measured by our prayers, then how small does that makes us feel? The practice of prayer in our crowded, daily lives can slip into the mundane, routine run of things: a tired, repetitive reeling off a list of those whom we know to be sick. And that's perfectly correct, of course, but are they the only ones we think stand in need of prayer? Just how unimaginative is our appreciation of God's grace? Suppose we were to make a list of all the sick people that it's recorded that the Apostle Paul prayed for. It's not a long list, is it? Please don't write that off by saying, 'Ah, but he was an apostle, wasn't he?' Paul himself had a long-term sickness that wasn't cured, because it wasn't God's will to heal him. And that, if you're wondering, was only because God had something even better for Paul to experience than healing – check it out from Second Corinthians chapter 12 (vv.9,10) – all about how Paul later fully acknowledged God's way was best.

Instead, whenever Paul brought people to mind, say in his opening greetings in one of his Bible letters, he demonstrated a keen insight into God's grace in the lives of his friends. If he caught them expressing genuine love to each other, Paul rightly saw that as an outflow of God's grace in their lives (Colossians 1:4). Instinctively, it seems, he bowed his head and thanked God for that, and then asked that it'd become more and more evident (Philippians 1:9). If, as he wrote, he understood his friends had their backs to the wall against extreme persecution, his first reaction wasn't to ask God for the immediate removal of that fierce opposition (2 Thessalonians 1:4). Paul had a mature insight into God's ways of grace, learnt in first-hand personal experience. Paul reminds them that recompense was on its way, but his immediate response was to bend his knee in prayer with thankfulness that their endurance was a display of their God-given worthiness as those called into God's kingdom – and this was something that was a tangible witness to the world at large.

When Paul writes to a young pastor struggling to navigate a myriad of pastoral dilemmas, it's as if his quill starts to flow with golden ink as he turns it all into praise of God the eternal king, the only wise God, who's the source of the wisdom - and everything else - the young pastor needs (1 Timothy 1:17).

For those in any affliction, Paul prayed they'd sense the closeness of God; his comfort, as he talked of it – and we understand that the gist of this comfort, as Paul's precise selected word makes clear, is that it comes from the Lord coming alongside us (2 Corinthians 1:1-11). For Paul, Christianity could be summed up as God's grace seen as faith working through love in the Christian community (Galatians 5:6). He was always on the lookout for signs of it in the everyday lives of his friends, and this gave him large scope for his prayers. We see Paul's spirituality shining through his prayer concerns, often bringing together in the varied texts of our Bible, the repeated themes of his joy, his thankfulness, and his prayers for a more abundance grace (Philippians 1:2-5). In short, as you'll have guessed, I find myself in agreement with Packer that our prayer agenda is the measure of our spirituality.

Where I'm leading to in all of this is to make the point that Bible-informed praying will be our best guide to help us, like Paul, to enlist goals in prayer that are more according to God's will and purposes, more in line with his values, in conformity with his character, while claiming his promises.

Getting to know God better, and praying better, are things that belong together. Another way of saying that is to say that prayer is a fruit born out of our relationship with God. We'd expect that, wouldn't we? After all, at a human level, in our relationships think of how your conversation with a long-standing friend with whom you've shared many experiences is so much more enriching and interesting than a fleeting conversation with someone you hardly know. In that latter circumstance, how can the communication be anything other than superficial: at best a polite and brief formality?

So, if our greatest need is to know God better, and this corresponds with praying better, let's see if the Lord will use Paul's Bible writings to bring us that blessing, shall we? Paul was a veteran prayer warrior - what does he teach us about the place of prayer in our lives? The Lord's public prayers on earth included the benefit of instructing others (John 11:42), and I believe he uses Paul's recorded prayers for that same purpose too. Let's take as an example a prayer of Paul's as recorded in 2 Thessalonians, and the first chapter, the first dozen or so verses:

> "Paul, Silas and Timothy,
>
> To the church of the Thessalonians in God our Father and the Lord Jesus Christ:

GET REAL ... LIVING EVERY DAY AS AN AUTHENTIC FOLLOWER OF CHRIST

Grace and peace to you from God the Father and the Lord Jesus Christ. We ought always to thank God for you, brothers and sisters, and rightly so, because your faith is growing more and more, and the love all of you have for one another is increasing. Therefore, among God's churches we boast about your perseverance and faith in all the persecutions and trials you are enduring.

All this is evidence that God's judgment is right, and as a result you will be counted worthy of the kingdom of God, for which you are suffering. God is just: He will pay back trouble to those who trouble you and give relief to you who are troubled, and to us as well. This will happen when the Lord Jesus is revealed from heaven in blazing fire with his powerful angels. He will punish those who do not know God and do not obey the gospel of our Lord Jesus. They will be punished with everlasting destruction and shut out from the presence of the Lord and from the glory of his might on the day he comes to be glorified in his holy people and to be marveled at among all those who have believed. This includes you, because you believed our testimony to you.

With this in mind, we constantly pray for you, that our God may make you worthy of his calling, and that by his power he may bring to fruition your every desire for goodness and your every deed prompted by faith. We pray this so that the name of our Lord Jesus may be glorified in you, and you in him, according to the grace of our God and the Lord Jesus Christ" (NIV).

First, I want us to observe the structure Paul uses here ('with this in mind,' 2 Thessalonians 1:11). In keeping with our earlier general remarks about Paul's prayer habits, he begins with thankfulness for signs of grace such as their growing faith, and their increasing love. Another outstanding feature of this prayer, and one we can surely learn from, is how Paul models for us how to reflect eternity's values. Prayer isn't simply about the here and now. We're conversing with the one who from everlasting to everlasting is God! It really helps to set out problems in the light of eternity as we order our prayer before God. Just the discipline of doing that often opens the door for the answering shift of perspective that is our basic need.

Now follows an example in 2 Thessalonians 1 of Paul offering a petition for his friends to become worthy of their calling, and of God's name and his love for them. How might we generalize this? Isn't it basically a prayer about becoming what we were not when the Gospel reached us? Notice this is NOT a prayer about God helping us to be successful, healthy, etc. How shallow such requests are – how they expose our small view of God. Lord, enlarge our prayers! What we really need is to become such persons now that we'll avoid shame at the future judgement-seat of Christ.

The Apostle John said he loved to hear of his children living out God's truth. Is that what thrills us about our family, or is it more the kind of job and salary and that new house or car that

GET REAL ... LIVING EVERY DAY AS AN
AUTHENTIC FOLLOWER OF CHRIST

tends to surface when we discuss them in conversation with others? Certainly, the Apostle John's focus would be on how they were doing spiritually, the other things being of a much lower order, interesting details as they are, of course. Prayer gets meaningful as we wrestle to surface our own desires to grow in the grace and knowledge of the Lord Jesus; and to become transformed by eradicating worldly desires as we seek the higher life in all its fulness (Colossians 3:1-5).

We can also follow Paul by requesting that God may facilitate our faith-prompted desires – bringing before him those neighbours we're witnessing to or that mission trip that's coming up. Finally, we end with the desire that God, not us, will be admired - it's about winning glory for him, not me. One coming day, we'll be glorified (perfectly holy at last) when we'll be just like him - that's God's long-term, good and personal plan for each of us – so why shouldn't we pray about its progress much more often in our prayers?

Surely, we'd give up praying, and Christianity itself, if we don't keep this perfected goal in sight. The discipline (and joy) of prayer is that it keeps this perspective uppermost in our minds when temporary disappointments come. I heard about a long-distance swimmer swimming in fog who gave up exhausted, and then discovered she'd very nearly reached her goal. What a different outcome if the sun had been shining. She'd have seen the endpoint drawing ever nearer and wouldn't have given up with so short a distance remaining. Prayer is vital because it's what keeps the end in sight for us.

I want to finish off on an even more practical note. I'm writing this in the Philippines where almost on a daily basis, in terms of the making of practical arrangements, I see my friends failing to plan and so planning to fail. So, we need to plan to pray. Set a definite time, don't just say 'later.' The Devil will make sure you won't find the time. He simply delights in seeing that our schedule gets too pressurized so we've got a legitimate excuse not to pray. It's vital for him that we don't pray. Even in private it's good to vocalize our prayer, as it tends to help us from drifting off into some daydream.

As a suggestion, based on what we've been saying: have you ever tried praying through the Psalms? Ambrose described them as a gymnasium for the soul. For added accountability, pray occasionally with a partner. And don't forget to make notes, prayer lists etc. A final word, because I know from experience it can sometimes be hard to get started, like trying to get a fire to kindle, the old Puritans used to say, 'Pray until you pray.' In other words, like an athlete pushing through the pain barrier, push yourself beyond dryness, beyond formalism ... Don't just ring the bell and run!

CHAPTER THREE: REALLY KNOWING GOD'S WILL THROUGH PRAYER

Perhaps more than anything else, John Knox is known for his prayer, "Give me Scotland, or I die." His was not an arrogant demand, but the passionate plea of a man willing to die for the sake of the pure preaching of the gospel and the salvation of his countrymen. Although Knox had been imprisoned and enslaved, and though he was often infirm and under threat of persecution, he lived out his theology: that "one man with God is always in the majority." As such, the prayers of one man heard at the throne of God were a threat to the throne of Scotland. During the time of the sixteenth-century Scottish Reformation, his ministry of preaching and prayer were so well known that (the Roman Catholic) Mary, Queen of Scots, is reputed to have said, "I fear the prayers of John Knox more than all the assembled armies of Europe."

That connection through prayer between earthly kingdoms and the realm of the heavens is testified to within the Bible itself. Daniel was a man whose prayers overturned world empires and advanced God's outstanding desire to dwell among men and women on earth who were obedient to his will. In the book of Daniel, chapter 10, there's exposed to us the reality of prayer in a fallen world. The rise and fall of world empires hinged on the prayers of one man then who was in touch with God by reading God's Word and by maintaining a daily prayer discipline. He still observed the daily rhythm of temple service timings decades after the temple had ceased to exist, obliterated by the disobedience of his compatriots.

Being surrounded by failure gives us no excuse whatever to relax our personal convictions. Daniel is three times described as someone whom God greatly esteemed. No honour attained in the empires of this world can rival that. The Lord explained to Daniel how the timings of his prayers coincided with major power-shifts on earth that in turn reflected developments in angelic conflicts in the spiritual arena. This tiny glimpse underlines how little we perceive of all that's entailed in our prayers.

And yet we can sometimes be tempted to wonder if prayer does change things. And if it does change things, then what exactly is it that it changes? "Does prayer change God's mind?" "No." The Bible says there are certain things God has decreed from all eternity. Those things will inevitably come to pass - regardless of 'pleading the blood', 'claiming the name', 'binding demonic forces' or whatever other unbiblical practice.

No human being has ever had a more profound understanding of divine sovereignty than Jesus. No man has ever prayed more effectively. In Gethsemane, he requested an option, a different way. When the request was denied, he bowed to the Father's will. In Matthew's Gospel, that sense of progression is conveyed to us in the way that the main clause changes when we go from the first to the second of our Lord's recorded prayers. "Let this cup pass away" (Matthew 26:39) in the first prayer becomes "Your will be done" (Matthew 26:42) in the second. The thrust of the prayer of our Lord thus changed from "If it is possible ..."

to "If it is not possible ..." The Lord was bowing to, and never attempting to bend, what was already settled from the counsels of eternity.

But then we may well react, as we grapple with a sense of reality in prayer, if God has it all settled is it not pointless to pray? Obviously, it can't be: otherwise why would he command us to pray? He also invites us to make our requests known. More than that, the assurance of the Scriptures is that prayer works: "The prayer of a righteous person has great power as it is working" (James 5:16). The problem is that we're not all that righteous. We could do with being a lot more like Daniel and Elijah when it comes to prayer. That brings us back round to our question: 'does prayer change things?' What prayer most often changes is us! That alone is reason enough to pray.

But still, the question is a troubling one: "If God knows everything, why pray?" The question assumes that prayer is one-dimensional and is defined simply as supplication or intercession. On the contrary, prayer is multidimensional. God's sovereignty casts no shadow over the prayer of adoration. God's foreknowledge or determinate counsel doesn't negate the prayer of praise. The only thing it should do is give us greater reason for expressing our adoration for who God is.

There is a certain sense in which God's sovereignty should influence our attitude toward prayer, at least with respect to adoration. If anything, our understanding of God's sovereignty should promote in us an intense prayer life of thanksgiving. Because of such knowledge, we should see that every benefit, every good and perfect gift, is an expression of the abundance of his grace. The more we understand God's sovereignty, the more our prayers will be filled with thanksgiving. And, more than that, in what way could God's sovereignty negatively affect the prayer of confession? I may not understand the relationship between divine sovereignty and human responsibility, but surely I realize that the failures I'm confessing have been brought about by my own will?

We ask again, does prayer change things? "Yes!" We only have to remember the biblical example of Nineveh. When God hangs his sword of judgment over people's heads, and they repent, he then withholds his judgment. That must mean that he's changed his mind, mustn't it? Not at all. The mind of God doesn't change, for God doesn't change. Things change – and they do so according to God's sovereign will - through secondary means in which prayer plays a part. In Nineveh's case, it was the timing of its judgement (see the book of Nahum). As we saw from Daniel, the prayer of his people is one of the things God uses to make things happen in this world.

To believe in the sovereignty of an unchanging God is no deterrent to prayer. In reality, the very reason we pray is because of God's sovereignty. Does prayer change God's mind? No. Does prayer change things? Yes, of course.

We need to make sure we're looking at this whole issue of prayer and God's will in a proper biblical way. The problem is we may mean different things when we use the general term 'the will of God.' The Bible, in fact, uses this expression 'the will of God' in at least three quite different ways, and we're going to need to distinguish between them if we want to get to the bottom of the question of prayer and the will of God.

When, earlier, we used the sacred example of our Lord in Gethsemane's garden, and we brought to mind his wording 'Your will be done,' we should clarify that as being what we might call the 'decretive' will of God. Now that's not an everyday word, is it, so it calls for some explanation. This is the will of God as having to do with his eternal decrees. These decrees are eternal, they're fixed, and our prayers aren't going to change them. The Lord himself left us the perfect example of how we interact in prayer with God's decrees. We bow to them in and through prayer, and on our part come to adore the God who willed it that way, for it's best – and so we should never want it changed.

Take as an example the return of our Lord. He's told us he's coming back (John 14:3); that is God's will and it's going to happen. How foolish then it would be for us to try to pray against the Lord's return!

A second way the words 'the will of God' are used in the Bible is when the Lord is prescribing how we should serve him. For example, it's God's will that we should be baptized, as that was clearly commanded in the Bible's historical account of how Christianity began. It's a command and practice that's recorded so consistently, without ambiguity as to its timing and manner, and recorded so uniformly as a practice in all the primitive churches, that we cannot escape into the opinion that this is only description for then, and not the will of God for all Christians today. But that's simply one example. There are a host of other commands: to love one another; to avoid stealing and lies and immorality and so on ... That's God's preceptive will for us. We describe it that way because it's comprised of all his precepts or commands detailing how he wills for us to live. These, and much more, are all contained in 'the Faith once for all delivered to the saints' (Jude v.3).

That, too, sounds rather non-negotiable, doesn't it? It would again be nonsense to pray about whether we might be granted special permission to sleep with someone who's not our own husband or wife! Once again, prayer cannot change God's will in that preceptive sense, any more than prayer cannot change God's will in its decretive sense. We can – and must – still pray in relation to these precepts, but in the same way as the Psalmist, confessing his failure to fully keep them, and asking God to incline his heart to do much better.

Finally, at least for our simple consideration, we come to the third way in which we can legitimately understand what God's will means in Scripture. It's well-known that 1 Timothy 2:4 speaks about it being God's will that all people will be saved. Does this mean we all need to be universalists? That is, those who believe (wrongly as it turns out, see Matthew 25:41,46) that ultimately everyone will be spared the judgement of the lake of fire. The Bible gives us explicit examples of specific persons who'll be banished there for ever (Revelation 20:10), so we know the universalist position is simply and totally wrong. So, what does it mean when we're told God wills all to be saved? The answer is found in the fact that elsewhere the Bible teaches us that God takes no pleasure in the death of the wicked (Ezekiel 33:11). Jesus lamented over the refusal of the city-dwellers of Jerusalem to come to him and find salvation

(Matthew 23:37). The clear sense is that God does not desire that anyone should be lost.

In Romans chapter 10, Paul prayed for his compatriots' salvation. He desired it - in fact he was most passionate about it. When I preach the message of salvation it's my desire people will be saved. At times, with persons well-known and perhaps related to us, we approach the intensely passionate desire that Paul expressed for their salvation. We are entering in a small way into God's desire for their salvation.

When our praying engages with things that belong within this category of God's will, we allow ourselves to be influenced through the practice of God's presence until our desires reflect his desires (Psalm 37:4). When we pray specifically for someone's salvation, our prayer encroaches upon the territory of God's (unknown) decrees - when Paul prayed generally for the unsaved (Romans 10:1) it was specific only in that the elect may obtain salvation (Acts 13:48).

Sometimes God permits a variation on the indicated timing of matters within his decretive will (Jeremiah 18:1-12; Amos 7:1-8; Exodus 32:10-14); at other times he uses those who set aside his preceptive will (e.g. by acts of murder) to bring about his decrees (but without endorsing their actions).

There are times when God wants us at a certain place, doing a certain thing, such as the biblical example of the so-called "Macedonian call" (Acts 16:6-10). We can also think of Philip (Acts 8:26) and of Peter and Ananias (Acts 10:1-23). However, this is in relation to knowing God's personal guidance in our lives, and it doesn't violate any of the 'wills' we've considered. I hope what we've said here helps to make clearer the difference between personal guidance and the biblical will of God.

CHAPTER FOUR: REALLY LIVING WITH INTEGRITY AT HOME (PART 1)

They say that 'charity begins at home.' I guess the implication is that our home life is the ultimate test. It's there we're observed most closely, and where our inconsistencies may be all too apparent. The Apostle John's biblical test to check if anyone's love for God was real was to observe whether that same person loved his brothers and sisters. Although that setting may be more the family of God rather than specifically their own natural family, the same principle applies, does it not? And our home life is linked to our church life, for Timothy received instructions from Paul that a man wasn't to be recognized as a church leader unless he'd proved himself in the domestic sphere. His home life had to be beyond reproach. And really these are standards that all believers should be aspiring to. Peter specifically says of women that their home life was to be such that unbelieving husbands would be won for the Lord simply by the conduct of their wives - without even a word needing to be spoken! (1 Peter 3:1).

We're meant to learn from the Bible story-line as well as from its direct commands. And woven into its text, we find details of the homes of some of its characters. They are of timeless application in terms of the truths they expose to us. Briefly, let's check out some examples.

There's the perennial danger of over-commitment outside the home. A parent preoccupied with the busy demands of professional life, and who doesn't put in special effort to balance that, might expect to lose the respect of his children. Try asking Eli the priest about that. Problems here were compounded by the fact that he couldn't effectively say 'no' to his kids. Unchecked by effective parental restraint, they grew up to be wilfully disobedient, their lives a total disaster area. From the stories of both David and Eli we can observe the effects of professional neglect on family life.

There's a terrible danger in parents being overcommitted outside the home and as a result not being available to give consistent input to their children's training. Sometimes rich, successful parents sit by their garden swimming pools and wonder why their son or daughter prefers to live in squalor down in a nearby commune. Maybe they feel more valued there. Parents can be preoccupied with providing a degree of lifestyle where material things take over. No amount of material things can compensate for an absent Dad, or Mum. What price the rough and tumble a toddler has with his Dad; building rapport which can be cashed in on later? The Bible perspective can be found in Psalm 127: "Children are a heritage from the LORD, the fruit of the womb is a reward. Like arrows in the hand of a warrior, so are the children of one's youth. Happy is the man who has his quiver full of them." In the ups and downs of daily domestic bliss (if that's not an oxymoron), this is a healthy reminder that children are a precious gift from God, a trust given into our charge, and our supreme task is to equip them to hit the mark in divine service.

GET REAL ... LIVING EVERY DAY AS AN AUTHENTIC FOLLOWER OF CHRIST

By contrast, the home of Obed-edom must have seemed like a genuinely God-fearing home. Why else would king David have permitted the Ark of the Covenant to have lodged there in the home of a foreigner? The ark of the Lord, the symbol of the Lord's presence, was now in that dear man's home. What a witness that would have been to the neighbourhood! Did people pop in to see the ark of the testimony which normally was only seen by the high priest of Israel? And if "Christ is settled down and at home in our hearts through faith" (Ephesians 3:17), will our lives not equally express the fear of the Lord and be powerful in their witness among our neighbours? Surely they will.

Then there's Lot who succeeded in business, but at the expense of his family. How come? Because he had the wrong emphasis – early in life his choices showed that he valued material success above spiritual success; that was way before he chose to bring up his children in the wrong environment. Seemingly he thought his children could live in Sodom and not be affected by it. It seems he thought his family would follow his instructions; instead they adopted the standards of their peers. It's dangerous for any parent to underestimate the power of the surrounding culture (Genesis 19:4-5). Outside of parental influence, the four greatest influences in a young person's home life are their peers, the internet, media and music.

How well Daniel's parents had moulded his value system in years of early training so that he could stand firm and loyal to his principles when he suddenly found himself in a big city and in a foreign culture surrounded by lots of temptations.

Job is a shining example to us of the need to pray for our kids lifelong. Job chapter 1 tells us he offered sacrifices regularly just in case any of his children had sinned against God. Some parents even have a day of prayer and fasting each week for their children, seeking God's guidance for them in their careers and relationships. As well as like Job in being conscious of his children's shortcomings, we can also ask God to help us in our own shortcomings as parents. We can regularly request that he'll compensate for our weaknesses and failings in a way that will ensure those young charges he's entrusted to us will not be damaged in any way, and we'll want to ask him to preserve them from the evil influences of the world, won't we? Yes, prayer is so vital!

It's good to read through the Bible's family histories with a parent's eye and a heart that's open to learn from the bad examples as well as the good. Again, we can see the bad results of favouritism from Isaac and Rebekah's family. We need to be open to all God can teach us through His Word in these days when the prevailing ideas of secularism put the family so much at risk. I'm referring to the attitude of being sceptical of religious instruction; the notion that there are no absolute values, rights or wrongs; and individualism – the put-yourself-first mentality. These all erode family life at home. God's wisdom for family life may not always be fashionable but it's never dated. A growing body of social research shows that such things as 2-parent families, marital fidelity, fatherhood and parental authority, together with faith in God are all highly beneficial factors in the well-being of families today. And no wonder, for that's what the Bible teaches!

In addition to examples, there's clear instruction also, of course. Family units were God's way of building society from the very beginning. And the Bible isn't lacking when it comes to finding detail on how to go about living successfully at home. In fact, God's Word clearly specifies the following ingredients: instruction (Deuteronomy 6:6-7); training (Proverbs 22:6); provision (2 Corinthians 12:14); nurturing (Ephesians 6:4); discipline (1 Timothy 3:4); and above all, love (Titus 2:4).

In fact, Deuteronomy chapter 6 starts off where that list has ended. Perhaps, best of all, it sets the tone for family life at home. God prefaced his remarks there by saying: "You shall love the LORD your God with all your heart, with all your soul, and with all your strength." What does this say to us? Only that in family life the paramount thing is love for God. It's God's will that the lives of parents be permeated with love for Him. And love for God will overflow into love for others too. The atmosphere in a Christian home should be loving. It recalls for me the touching tenderness of God's language towards Israel, called Ephraim in Hosea chapter 11 verse 3.

God says: "I taught Ephraim to walk, taking them by their arms ... I drew them with gentle cords.' Some versions have it that God took them on His arms. Any parent can relate to God's description here of gently, tenderly, assisting a toddler to take those first faltering steps. With real affection and satisfaction and pleasure the parent says, 'Well done!' Sometimes it'll require to be tough love when correction needs to be applied, for read on in Hosea to find out how God's love isn't an indulgent, sentimental thing. Far from it! Hebrews 12 and 6 confirms that "whom the LORD loves He chastens". The important thing for us to imitate is that even his disciplines are full of love.

What we're saying is God's love must be uppermost in family life, and we're saying that on the authority of Deuteronomy chapter 6. We need to put first what God puts first. If God doesn't have the first place in our lives, then our children will be quick to spot the hypocrisy when we attempt to teach them spiritual values. We need to pass down to our children a healthy reverence for God as well as an attentive ear to obey his voice.

There's the need to impart more than words of instruction but also our own values, our own selves - which had been Paul's example in the case of his parental-type love for the Thessalonian church (1 Thessalonians 2:8). Deuteronomy 6 verse 6, which we mentioned, says: "And these words which I command you today shall be in your heart." How important that is! Just as parents' hearts are to be permeated with God's love, here we have another fundamental principle for our life at home. There's little chance of children becoming gripped by God's Word and the reality of God if their parents don't display it. The hearts of parents are to be captivated with the truth of God and his Word. Many things are 'caught' by our children rather than explicitly 'taught' to them. If we say Christianity is very important but don't go to church gatherings, they'll actually learn that Christianity isn't important. The same will happen if we teach the importance of faith but then worry about everything ourselves. If we piously talk about taking our problems to the Lord but then make our own independent decisions, again the effect will be opposite to what's desired. If we say money isn't very important but then ourselves live materialistically, it'll be very unlikely that they'll get the message.

Imparting our own selves to them is a costly thing in terms of time. The old adage about quality time being more important than quantity time is probably not as true as we'd like to believe when we lead busy lives. Suffice it to say that it's important we spend blocks of time with our children. Maybe we can watch their favourite TV programme with them and creatively use it as a discussion topic to casually debrief them on any media message that's been put over. By the way, I say 'casually' to indicate a natural, chatty style of dialogue with our children as together we review the content of TV or radio programmes, or magazine features. But I certainly don't mean 'casual' as implying it's not too important to monitor the values children get taught through the media - on the contrary, I think it's extremely important to expose whatever values aren't biblical values, especially when sinful behaviours - like violence and immorality - are being glamourized.

While we're thinking of young family members being impressionable, it's worth noting that in the Bible's inspired advice to parents in Deuteronomy 6 verse 7, it stresses the need for parents 'impressing' or 'teaching diligently' God's commands to their children. Literally, it might have been translated 'you shall intensely sharpen your children' which serves to show that the type of teaching God has in mind is active communication of his truth and values, not passive. Certainly, the transfer of truth from one generation to the next is not automatic, but requires time and effort. Time and effort that has to be supplied by parents, who themselves have God's truth at the core of their beings, and allow it to become woven into the fabric of their existence.

Proverbs 22 and 6 is a great verse in the Bible on the training of children within a family. It says: "Train up a child in the way he should go" or "Train up a child according to his way". The second translation acknowledges that each child is different. That's something that's been brought home to me since the birth of our second child. Even from a few months Anna bore the stamp of her own personality - quite different from Michael her older brother in her sleep patterns, eating habits, manners and in the way she reacts to people. In training them it's important to be sensitive to their different, God-given characteristics. When it says "train a child according to his way" the word 'way' literally means something trodden. Elsewhere in the Bible it crops up in different connections as in the effect of someone treading on a bow in order to bend it to shape. That's quite enlightening as we link it back to our child-rearing verse - it relates to how each child's personality is shaped differently. We wouldn't necessarily expect to bring up all our children in exactly the same way: for example some may respond better to encouragements than warnings or vice versa.

The second point on the training of children that flows directly from an understanding of the same Bible verse in Proverbs 22 has to do with the fact that the word 'train' comes from a word referring to the roof of the mouth, and was used to describe the action of a midwife dipping her fingers into the juice of crushed dates and then massaging a child's gums and palate. The tangy taste stimulated the child to suck. There's a wide-ranging principle we can take from this, that the parents (not exclusively the mother by any means) in training their children, must strive to cultivate a thirst in their child for wholesome things.

Think of the words of Philippians 4 and 8: "Whatever things are true, whatever things are noble, whatever things are just, whatever things are pure, whatever things are lovely, whatever things are of good report, if there is any virtue and if there is anything praiseworthy - meditate on these things.' If we as parents don't demonstrate such superb family values, but say watch any old trash on the television, then it's not very likely our children will acquire a taste for those praiseworthy things of Philippians 4. Above all, parents are to seek to stimulate a real thirst for God and his truth. Many Christian parents have their own stories of their very young children sitting with their little kiddies' Bible - like the eight-year-old found sitting in the living room reading her little devotional. 'What are you doing?', she was asked by someone. 'I'm pretending to be Mummy', came the reply.

Mothers, especially, have a tremendous responsibility and privilege in moulding the generation to come, particularly at an early stage when the clay, so to speak, is still wet and impressionable. What's the saying? 'Give me a child till he's 7', is it, "and I'll show you the man'. That could be a very loose paraphrase of our Bible text from Proverbs! There was a former President of the United States who allegedly passed folks in the street without so much as a second glance, but on encountering a child, he would stop and doff his hat, because, he explained, who knows what that child will become. It's an awesome thought, isn't it? Parents, mothers, you are raising tomorrow's leaders. What an impact on history unassuming mothers like Susannah Wesley have had! Who would dare say theirs was a wasted life!

CHAPTER FIVE: REALLY LIVING WITH INTEGRITY AT HOME (PART 2)

The virtuous woman of Proverbs chapter 31 gives us a biblical example of selfless and self-sacrificing behaviour putting the good of others in the family first. Even in introducing her in verse 10 by saying "her worth is far above rubies", we get a hint that there's something much more important in family life than money and materialism. By the way, talking of her worth, do we aim to build up the self-esteem of those in the family around us? Some Christians say they have a difficulty with terms like 'self-esteem' or 'self-image', and they can so easily be tainted with selfish pride, but basically all I mean by building self-esteem is: do we pass on encouragement and appropriate compliments in order to help each family member feel valued and worthwhile, as this woman did in Proverbs 31? Listen:

> "Her children rise up and call her blessed; her husband also, and he praises her: 'Many daughters have done well, but you excel them all.' Charm is deceitful and beauty is passing, but a woman who fears the LORD, she shall be praised. Give her of the fruit of her hands, and let her own works praise her in the gates."

Verse 11 says "the heart of her husband safely trusts her". Hers was a life of transparent integrity. This woman was a help and confidant to her husband who held a responsible position. And so we come to verse 15 which tells us "she also rises while it is yet night, and provides food for her household." Talk about selfless diligence - she knew all about it! She's got a regular 'cottage industry' going here in Proverbs 31:

> "She seeks wool and flax, and willingly works with her hands. She is like the merchant ships, she brings her food from afar ... She considers a field and buys it; from her profits she plants a vineyard ... She perceives that her merchandise is good, and her lamp does not go out by night. She stretches out her hands to the distaff, and her hand holds the spindle. She extends her hand to the poor, yes, she reaches out her hands to the needy. She is not afraid of snow for her household, for all her household is clothed with scarlet ... She makes linen garments and sells them, and supplies sashes for the merchants ... She watches over the ways of her household, and does not eat the bread of idleness."

I can believe that! There was no room for idleness in her life. And the picture I get is not one of stress and conflict of interest between home and career. Rather it's the picture of a wife and mother fulfilled in the use of her skills and talents, yet whose family comes first - a real 'worker at home' as Paul described Christian women to Titus in chapter 2 verse 5. Here was someone committed to her family's well-being and taking domestic responsibilities seriously, while at the same time trading profitably in a successful business enterprise. We see this especially in her skilful provision of food and clothing for her family. She'd got the balance right, without sacrificing anything of her dignity as a person, as a woman, and as a wife and mother. In fact, what we find here is the idea of a gracious mother. Overall the chapter describes her with strong arms, open hands reaching out, clothed with dignity, speaking kindness, fearing the Lord, praised by her works and acclaimed by her family. Her children would grow up, of course ...

And as our children get older, the challenges can increase. There can be a tendency for a parent to wish to fulfil his or her own dreams through the children rather than let them be what they want to be and are suited for. And sometimes our own youthful and reckless experiences can fill us with quite unjustified suspicions and fears about their intentions as they become more independent. I wonder if at least a part of Saul's jealousy of David might have been due to his frustration that it wasn't his own son Jonathan who defeated the giant and led the army out to battle. It seems clear that we need to let children find their own niche and encourage them at what they're naturally good at.

Jephthah, of whom we read in Judges chapter 11, is an example of someone who didn't fit in at home. In fact he was driven out of the family home. What a tragedy, for he quickly got in with the wrong crowd who gave him the kind of acceptance and esteem he never enjoyed at home. It's sad today to talk to young people who have effectively been driven from home by well-meaning but misunderstanding parents. It would break their heart to realize that their son or daughter's foolish behaviour -

which they find so hurtful - was due in part at least to their mismatched expectations or unrealistic ambitions for their child.

Well now, we've thought about the woman in the family from the point of view of Proverbs chapter 31, so it would be good to look at the man in the family as viewed from Psalm 112:

> "Blessed is the man who fears the LORD, who delights greatly in His commandments. His descendants will be mighty on earth; the generation of the upright will be blessed. Wealth and riches will be in his house, and his righteousness endures forever. Unto the upright there arises light in the darkness; He is gracious, and full of compassion, and righteous. A good man deals graciously and lends; he will guide his affairs with discretion. Surely he will never be shaken; the righteous will be in everlasting remembrance. He will not be afraid of evil tidings; his heart is steadfast, trusting in the LORD … He has dispersed abroad, he has given to the poor; his righteousness endures forever." (NKJV)

What comes across straightaway is an emphasis on being God-fearing, righteous and upright. But, we ask, how can this form of spiritual authenticity come about? How can we better ensure that our domestic lives are like this? What was the very first thing said about the man in Psalm 112? "Blessed is the man who fears the LORD, who delights greatly in His commandments." Surely this is the heart of the matter and is cultivated by spending time daily as a family around the open Bible in the home, perhaps at the meal table. Not that we should attempt to impart eternal truths to youngsters in unending devotions.

No, we need to be fairly brief, illustrative and ready with relevant applications for their age level. What can be better for the family unit than if, after the homespun chat across the meal table, we bring our family matters to God. Here the genuine Christianity of parents can and will be proved as we bring our family decisions and problems before God and then thank him together for his help once we receive it. God will be seen to be real in our lives and not just a topic in church. The parent's authentic example will set a foundational example for the children's lifestyle - one in which it will be natural to talk about God and to God.

Proverbs 24 verses 3 and 4: "Through wisdom a house is built, and by understanding it is established; by knowledge the rooms are filled with all precious and pleasant riches.' Of course, this is not so much the house but the home and its various relationships that are being built up - and whose building or development requires wisdom, understanding and knowledge. 1 Peter 3:1-6 seems to give us building bricks for a successful home life. Check it out, and you may be able to confirm mention of respectful faithfulness; being careful with appearance and attitude; submissiveness through paying close attention to the other; making the right response to a loving initiator; living without being over-committed outside the marriage; reading the mood signals; and honouring with respect and appreciation. Wise couples will be alert to our proneness to self-centredness, and ...

Parental wisdom will express itself as occasion arises in wise forms of discipline of the children in the home. But we must be in total control of ourselves whenever we discipline our children. Understanding and knowledge come into play, too, in discerning between an undesirable act and a direct challenge to parental authority. We found it good advice in our experience of young children not to turn mealtimes into battlegrounds. A child cannot be scolded into eating. There's no point in fighting a losing battle and meals are cases in point where the child's stubborn will may easily get the upper hand. It's better to say, "Okay you can leave your dinner if you wish. But listen, there are no sweets and biscuits before tea-time". Then, at tea-time, you re-heat and re-serve what was left over from dinner time. If the child doesn't listen to Mum or Dad, he or she will soon listen to a rumbling tummy! Another undesirable act where punishment isn't appropriate is in the case of breakages occurring during play. Correction is necessary, though, when a child retorts: 'I will not' or 'shut up'.

Wise parents build their family life with lots of loving esteem, open communication and fair discipline. And discipline needs to be fair to be effective. Inconsistent discipline will make a child insecure, whereas children want consistent discipline - there's security in knowing where the boundaries are. When children 'test the limits', we might think of what they're doing as being like a security officer trying all the doors of a building hoping to find them safely locked - just checking. When youngsters get older they can even be invited to participate in setting the rules. The rules then become 'theirs' and strangely they're often stricter than we would've dared to be! We can also work with them at associating privilege with responsibility. To sum up, with discipline, children are entitled to know what the rules are in advance; to have correction privately administered; with the violation and its consequence clearly explained; and to be assured of our loving concern for them at all times.

I'm so grateful for that short verse in Luke 2:52 that says, "Jesus increased in wisdom and stature, and in favour with God and men". As a holy teenager He underwent mental, physical, spiritual and social development. The teenage years for all of us are years when we benefit from lots of reassurance and unconditional love. Keeping our expectations as parents realistic and affirming and accepting our kids can help prevent them looking to negative methods of getting attention from their peers.

It's useful to check out more of the great resource of parental wisdom that's to be found in Proverbs. There a father talks to his son. Some 14 times in the first 7 chapters we come across the words 'my son' prefacing some timeless piece of fatherly instruction. There's warning against keeping the wrong sort of company as well as against laziness and immorality; but also encouragement to seek God's guidance and to be wise.

If you find living the Christian life very difficult because not everyone at home is a Christian, let me just say that I remember hearing a delightful meditation on the Lord Jesus' own home circumstances. The speaker felt a window was opened on the Lord's home life when he said in Mark 6:4 that "Only in his home town among his relatives and in his own house is a prophet without honour." The occasion was the Lord's second rejection at Nazareth where he'd been brought up. Perhaps the sadness in his voice that day could almost be felt. Divisions in the home had cut him keenly and the hurts of some 20 or more years surface in this remark. Christian, take heart - he knows what it's like to have a difficult daily life at home. And human nature being what it is, we can well imagine his half-brothers being resentful of their perfect older brother. So, if yours is a divided home, speak to him about your problems in the confidence that he, too, has experienced them first-hand.

And we can learn from Christ's example. I'd say that, towards the end of Ephesians chapter 4, we can find five tips that apply to our home life, because they stem from what it means to learn Christ. Again, I'd ask you to look it up and discover for yourself the requirement to speak truth (including to say what you mean); not becoming sinfully angry (and then only briefly); being totally honest and trustworthy due to being other-centred; guarded in speech by the Spirit's control which instructs us to encourage others; to avoid bitterness and slander as we attempt to display tender-heartedness instead.

CHAPTER SIX: REALLY GROWING AS PART OF A LOCAL CHURCH

It's been said that, 'In every local church community there is comedy and tragedy, companionship and loneliness, conflict and love. On this side of Christ's return, it will always be so. But God still uses congregations to reach the world, sanctify one another, and work out his divine plan of redemption' (Christianity Today, April 2016).

Before he went to the cross, the one whom all Christians claim to follow prayed a prayer that's recorded in John's Gospel in which he asked his Father that the sequel to his dying on the cross might be a genuine community of Christians. Although this was a prayer of global proportions, the headline qualities that Christ passionately desired to see in any local grouping of his followers were: truth, unity, mission and holiness. Although applying in scope to the whole movement that would carry his name, they must first and last apply at street level in all the local churches that integrate within the community he reached out for in prayer.

Christianity is to be a movement in two dimensions. First, we're called out of the world to be worshippers whom his Father is seeking. This should mean we're to be much more seeker-sensitive to the Father, than seeker-sensitive to other would-be worshippers. Second, we're sent outwards into this world to be his witnesses; which means we're to be not so much church-centred as we are God-centred. It's about being outward-looking: a people who are welcoming, accessible, the very embodiment of the gospel; and demonstrating the values of God's kingdom in this world.

Christianity, as should be immediately obvious from even a superficial reading of the New Testament, is something that can't be done on a purely individualistic basis. It demands a corporate expression. Nowhere is this more practically underlined than by the repeated occurrence of a single word in the original Bible language. For the sake of the record, it's a single word in Greek: ἀλλήλων (ah-LAY-loan), but expressed in English as 'one another.' It's used 100 times in 94 New Testament verses. 47 of those verses give instructions to people in local churches, and 60% of those instructions come to us through the Apostle Paul. When you look at these verses, a few common themes show up.

Something like one third of these 'one-another commands' deal with the unity of each local church (Mark 9:50; John 6:43; Romans 12:16; 15:5, 7; 1 Corinthians 11:33; Galatians 5:15, 26; Ephesians 4:2, 32; Colossians 3:13; 1 Thessalonians 5:15; James 4:11; 5:9, 16). In detail, they tackle issues like: being at peace, not grumbling, being of the same mind, accepting, not envying or boastfully challenging one another, but tolerating one another with gentle patience, above all being kind and forgiving without complaining far less taking revenge – instead seeking each other's good with personal confession when necessary, all without complaining.

GET REAL ... LIVING EVERY DAY AS AN AUTHENTIC FOLLOWER OF CHRIST

Then another third of them target love among Christians in local church life (John 13:34, 15:12,17; Romans 13:8; 1 Thessalonians 3:12, 4:9; 1 Pet.1:22; 1 Jn.3:11, 4:7, 11; 2 Jn. v.5). Again, in terms of the specifics, it's things like: acknowledging, serving and tolerating one another, all with real devotion.

Of the other third, half of them concern humility (Romans 12:10,16; Philippians 2:3; Galatians 5:13; John 13:14; Ephesians 5:21; 1 Peter 5:5). In other words, subjecting ourselves to serving each other, regarding the other person's needs as of a higher priority than our own, so giving preference to the other person. Besides all those, we've not to judge one another nor stumble but rather to encourage, speak the truth and to pray for each other (Romans 14:13; 27; 16:16; 1 Corinthians 16:20; 2 Corinthians 13:12; 1 Corinthians 7:5; Galatians 6:2; Ephesians 4:25; Colossians 3:9; 1 Thessalonians 4:18; 5:11; Hebrews 10:24; James 5:16; 1 Peter 4:9).

To help us visualize what all this looks like in practice, we find a ready, worked example from Christianity's earliest days. It's found in Acts 9:31. "So the church throughout all Judea and Galilee and Samaria enjoyed peace, being built up; and, going on in the fear of the Lord and in the comfort of the Holy Spirit, it continued to increase."

Okay, but what sort of upbuilding ministry is meant here? Edification is what we're talking about and it happens when the relevant range of the New Testament spiritual gifts are properly understood and put into operation locally (see Ephesians 4:12-13). In New Testament times, the range of these gifts found its biblical expression in churches of God, and led to their growth in spiritual maturity.

Next, the local church is to be a 'going concern.' We might compare it with an eastern shepherd who went out ahead of his sheep (John 10:4). There's a sense of movement, direction and going forward all contained in this word.

The Apostle Paul was forward-looking. We can see this as he prepared to hand the baton of ministry over to Timothy. I think Paul's pastoral letters to Timothy give us a balanced all-round view of the main goals of the local church in the distinct areas of its use of God's word, its worship, its work for God, its welfare, its witness and its warfare. Shall we briefly unpack those before returning to Acts 9?

There's a tremendous emphasis on the Word of God throughout the whole of this second letter to Timothy (1:13; 2:15; 3:16; 4:2). True Christian learning is to be a learning that lives.

Turning now to worship, there's a fair bit in First Timothy chapter 2 about our worshipful approach to God - about the reverence and orderliness that's required in our public drawing near to God.

Moving on to the topic of 'work', there can really be no doubting Paul's message that the local church is to be a place of work for all who are in it - and hard work at that, for Paul compares Christian service to the labour of a hard-working farmer (2:6). Among Paul's favourite words were those that stress the strong exertion required in Christian service.

GET REAL ... LIVING EVERY DAY AS AN AUTHENTIC FOLLOWER OF CHRIST

Then there's Paul's encouragement to Timothy to witness the good confession - to make confession of his faith in Christ. Just another reminder that we're all called to be witnesses of the Lord Jesus.

Regarding welfare, it's interesting to remember that we started out with the example of church life from Acts chapter 9, the same chapter which mentions the death of Dorcas and mentions 'all the widows' (v.39) at Joppa. Paul's pastoral letters give a clear indication of what's meant to be each local church's responsibility for the social welfare of all those belonging to its number, especially the needy. This is the duty of Christian care that's to be shown to all those who are in real need - first of all to any in the church. Care is to be an outstanding feature of church life, just as it marked out the first local church of God at Jerusalem, which was certainly one whose fellowship really functioned.

Paul also spoke to Timothy about warfare. Why? Because those in the local church come under attack from the world around - a world that makes assaults on a Christian lifestyle. These then are the main duties of a local church, such as those we remind ourselves of again from Acts 9:31 (NASB) ...

> "So the church throughout all Judea and Galilee and Samaria enjoyed peace, being built up; and, going on in the fear of the Lord and in the comfort of the Holy Spirit, it continued to increase."

What does it mean when it's described as going forward in the comfort of the Holy Spirit? The same word 'comfort' is used repeatedly by Paul near the beginning of his first letter to the Church of God at Corinth where it seems as if the presence of God among them was relieving their hurts as well as touching the lives of others through them. Their troubles had brought God close to them, made him very real to them, and they were enjoying the relief and encouragement his presence had brought. Having really sensed that themselves, they were now in a position to serve wider needs in their locality. When they came across neighbours or friends who were struggling, they now found they could dispense comfort to those others - from their own experience of knowing comfort when they'd been in difficulty.

When in trouble or needing help, we reach for our Bibles, and God through the ministry of his Word draws near for our help - maybe as the gift of another believer is used to share a spiritual message with us. How important it is that we show the reality of our faith, and of our walk with the Lord, by sharing the good things of his Word with each other. These are things that can really encourage and uplift. The word 'comfort' is used in this way too, when Paul says, again to his Christian friends at Rome: "... he who exhorts, in exhortation; he who gives, with liberality; he who leads, with diligence; he who shows mercy, with cheerfulness" (Romans 12:6-8 NKJV).

The gift described as 'exhorting' or 'comforting' is the gift of encouragement. I'm sure we've all known times when someone has just said the right thing to us at just the right time, and we found it to be a real encouragement from the Lord. This gift of encouragement has been translated as the gift of stimulating the faith of others. Remember it's the word 'comfort' still, and we began by thinking of a church that was growing because it was moving forward in the comfort of the Holy Spirit. We'd expect a church like that to be a church where faith was being stimulated, wouldn't we? But what does that look like? We'll look further into this in the next chapter.

CHAPTER SEVEN: REALLY ENCOURAGING AS PART OF A LOCAL CHURCH

This gift of encouragement has been translated as 'the gift of stimulating the faith of others'. Remember it's the word 'comfort' we're continuing to think of as we review the biblical church described for us in Acts 9:31, one that was growing because it was moving forward in "the comfort of the Holy Spirit". We saw before how the gift of exhorting is the gift of comforting. It's through this gift of exhortation that the Holy Spirit ministers comfort by uncovering and resolving problems that, if left, would prevent spiritual growth taking place among Christians.

When in trouble or needing help, we reach for our Bibles, and God through the ministry of his Word draws near to encourage us - perhaps using the gift of another believer to explain its spiritual message to us. The word 'comfort' is used in this way when Paul says, again to his Christian friends at Rome: "he who exhorts, in exhortation; he who gives, with liberality; he who leads, with diligence; he who shows mercy, with cheerfulness" (Romans 12:6-8 NKJV).

The gift described as 'exhorting' or 'comforting' is the gift of encouragement. Many things can hold us back, even as Christians. For some it may be an inability to overcome feelings of bitterness or resentment; for others it may be frustration that inclines to mild depression, or losing the battle with impure thoughts. Trying to change the way people behave isn't usually effective until they can be helped to change the way they think. And that's where this practical spiritual gift of encouragement comes in.

In a friendly and helpful way – in a way that's not unwelcome - the encourager begins to explore with the person concerned what their difficulty seems to be, gently asking probing questions and taking time to reflect back for confirmation of the answers. Active listening like this will come across as caring, accepting and sends the message that the person struggling is valued. As the conversation develops, the encourager, in a caring way, tunes into the person's negative feelings. Are they coming across as angry, or afraid or as feeling guilty? Those are the three tell-tale emotions.

Let's get very practical and look at an example. We'll take one involving a case when fear may be the emotion that presents itself. Suppose we've noticed that a Christian at church doesn't get involved with anything. As we show interest, and make ourselves available for an encouraging chat, we gradually pick up on the fact that they're not taking part in projects because they desperately want to steer clear of any responsibility - and that this is due to a fear of failure on their part. In helping them to see that this is, in fact, unbiblical behaviour, the encourager may begin to uncover long-standing opinions that the person holds of himself or herself. Maybe from earliest years they've been told, 'You're no good', 'You can't do that', 'Let me do it for you'. And so they've come to believe it and behave accordingly. An encourager can do no better than to emphasize that anything we can do as Christians is only in the strength the Lord provides (Philippians 4:13).

And the best way to encourage someone like that is by following the good advice of the Bible itself - as when James tells us to be good listeners - 'be swift to hear, slow to speak' (James 1:19), he says. And what an example is held up for us in Ezekiel, of whom the Bible says that when he was delivering his message 'he sat where they sat' (Ezekiel 3:15). It's true, isn't it, that people need to know how much we care before they care how much we know. They need to know we're on their side, and we need to show we can see the thing from their point of view too. God's own dealings with Jonah (Jonah 4:4) teaches us the value of asking sensitive but not intrusive questions; while Paul in writing to the Ephesians (4:15) reminds us to speak the truth only in love. The point is that if it's loving then it can be received.

In effect, we've just walked through four steps to problem-solving. Let me point them out, and hopefully it'll reinforce them in our minds. Stimulating someone's faith who appears to be flagging somewhat begins with listening. As we listen, we should cultivate the habit of reflecting back what we're picking up. This has a double advantage. First, it makes sure we are interpreting the vibes correctly. Second, it encourages the person we're listening to that someone is taking the time to focus on understanding them. By listening we're trying to identify the main emotion that's coming across, whether it's guilt, fear or anger. That, in turn, guided us to view their particular behaviour as a coping strategy. In reality, it's more than that, for it's a pain-relieving strategy also inasmuch as the motivation for what they're doing is that they're trying to fill the pain of coping with a deficit in one or other of their three basic needs. And these needs are self-worth, security and significance, that is: a sense of worth as a person; a sense of belonging to something we can identify with; and a sense of contributing in a meaningful way, so making a difference. It's when one of those basic emotional needs is not being met that we become tempted to adopt a strategy to compensate in some way, or at least to relieve the pain of that emotional loss.

The gifted encourager will then, fourthly and lastly, try to expose that behaviour to the person, in order to help them to see their need to turn from it, and instead to look to the Lord, depending on him primarily to meet all their needs. In summary, again, the encourager's strategy is:

   1. Listen and reflect with questions.

   2. Tune in to identify the emotion - whether anxiety/ fear or anger or guilt.

   3. Pinpoint the wrong, independent coping strategy (e.g. withdrawal), and ...

   4. Entice to repentance and dependence.

These are the steps an encourager takes when presented with someone who:

   a) Isn't finding all his or her basic needs (i.e. a sense of worth, belonging or making a meaningful contribution) being met; and as a result ...

b) Perceives a shortfall that in turn produces pain which demands relief.

c) The sinful tendency then is to develop our own independent coping (pain-relieving) mechanism;

d) ... which results in one of those three negative emotions (which was our starting point above).

I next want to suggest to you that we can picture the types of longings we all have as three concentric circles. We'll label them as deep, deeper, and deepest. We can bear deep or even deeper longings not being fulfilled in the measure that our deepest longings are energising our pursuit of God.

But if at that deepest level we turn to other pleasures, then the appetite for what only God can provide becomes a demanding tyrant (a 'god' in Philippians 3:18); and the drive for relief becomes a compulsive craving which can only block our trusting enjoyment of God.

Outside of Christ people are trying to fill the God-shaped-hole, the deepest longings, with things that can never satisfy. Christians are promised satisfaction of their innermost being in abundant measure, but there may be times when we don't enjoy the two outer levels of satisfaction in the painful context of this hurting world where things can and do still go wrong. Trials are designed, or at least permitted, so as to fuel our pursuit of God at the deepest level.

There's a lot of misconception about 'life in all its fulness,' as Jesus called it. Going back to our picture of three concentric circles, life in all its fulness is not about having all three levels of deep, deeper and deepest longings fulfilled in the here and now. The obedient Christian doesn't feel good all the time. We're not guaranteed sustained physical comfort (namely those deep longings), nor permanent satisfaction in our close relationships (that is, the fulfilment of the deeper longings). However, when we seek the Lord we're promised we'll find the sufficiency of his grace for now; and bright hope for tomorrow.

The deepest fullness can come through times of difficulty as we struggle with denied comfort and strained relationships. The springs of water bathing our deepest longings with his presence now and with his promises for later don't eliminate the pain of unmet desires at other levels. Merely focusing on relieving our pain leaves us in danger of straying from that path.

Thinking influences behaviour - as a man thinks so is he (Proverbs 23:7) – and it's important for the would-be encourager to realize that he or she can't change another person's behaviour without them first having their thinking changed. And our thinking needs to be changed so that we have the mind of Christ. On that point, I'd like to share what I call the S.I.M.P.L.E.S.T way to become what we are in Christ. It's how I now regard the process with the help of the Bible's teaching on it. The name 'simplest' is an acrostic, where each letter stands for a relevant word in the description of the method.

'S' stands for 'Spirit,' and the point to associate with this is that we must begin our quest by prayerfully orientating our human spirit to God's Spirit – for that's the way for us to receive God's communication (Romans 8:16; 1 Corinthians

2:12; Psalm 19:7), including the revelation of whom we are to become in Christ.

The I and the M stand for Intent of Mind. This describes reading the Scriptures intently – with the aim of rebooting our mind with the knowledge of truth (1 Timothy 2:4). It's in this way that we come to learn Christ (Ephesians 4:20), leaving behind previous futile forms of thinking.

So, S for Spirit, our own human spirit, and I M for Intent of Mind. Those are the first three letters of SIMPLEST. And next, the P stands for Penetrates the heart – which is what God's truth does when our mind is set on God's things. As we meditate on the Bible's teaching, committing to memory the truth set before our mind, its values then begin to filter down into the core of our being from where they can influence our lifestyle choices.

This is where we pick up the L and E of SIMPLEST, drawing them from the word, LifE. The heart, at the centre of our lives, is where we reflect on God's things with 'purpose of heart' until they come to shape our will (Proverbs 23:7), and we submit our 'mortified' body (Romans 12:1) as poised to do good, and for productive outcomes in our life. Our Soul's Transformation is now underway. By the way, that's the S T that completes our acronym: SIMPLEST – it's the S T from the initials of Soul's Transformation. We are now ready to display modified behaviour in the life of our soul – this being the result of processing our altered thinking (Romans 8; Colossians 3; 2 Peter 1; Galatians 5).

CHAPTER EIGHT: REALLY CONFIDENT AS PART OF A LOCAL CHURCH

Recently, a church survey on growing churches summed up one of its major findings with the headline: 'Confident churches grow'. Think of that for a moment alongside Proverbs 14:26 (NKJV), which says: "In the fear of the LORD there is strong confidence." Fear in this sense means 'reverence' rather than 'terror', of course. And the message here is that if we're reverencing God then there's really nothing we need to be afraid of in this life. Confidence, produced by a sense of the fear of the Lord, would have been the experience of the church throughout all Judea and Galilee and Samaria, which, you remember: "enjoyed peace, being built up; and, going on in the fear of the Lord and in the comfort of the Holy Spirit, it continued to increase" (Acts 9:31 NASB).

A holy boldness or confidence was something that did indeed characterize those early Christians. We even read of them "joyfully accepting the plundering of their goods" (Hebrews 10:34). I don't think we're left in any doubt that this was due to the fact that they'd a holy boldness towards God. It characterized their worship too in response to what we read in Hebrews 10:19:

> "Therefore, brothers, since we have confidence to enter the holy places by the blood of Jesus, by the new and living way that he opened for us through

> the curtain, that is, through his flesh, and since we have a great priest over the house of God, let us draw near with a true heart in full assurance of faith."

This confidence, or boldness, was seen too in the general level of their confident expression of Christian beliefs: "For we have come to share in Christ, if indeed we hold our original confidence firm to the end" (Hebrews 3:14). In Acts chapter 4, when the authorities "... saw the boldness of Peter and John, and perceived that they were uneducated, common men, they were astonished. And they recognized that they had been with Jesus." Even under threat, believers in Jerusalem are recorded as praying that 'with all boldness' they might be granted to speak the word of the Lord (Acts 4:29). The prayer was answered, and we read: "And when they had prayed, the place in which they were gathered together was shaken, and they were all filled with the Holy Spirit and continued to speak the word of God with boldness."

Isn't the lesson here that a boldness before God will produce a boldness before men and women? A church which serves in the fear of the Lord will be a church which confidently holds out the word of life. There's no doubt that that was the situation in Acts chapter 9 where we read of this expanding church going forward in the fear of the Lord. This expanding circle of believers, we've said, was going on in the fear of the Lord. But what does that mean in practical terms beyond the idea of giving a holy boldness, which we've just been briefly exploring?

Proverbs 8:13 (NKJV) defines the fear of the Lord when it tells us: "The fear of the LORD is to hate evil; pride and ar-

GET REAL ... LIVING EVERY DAY AS AN AUTHENTIC FOLLOWER OF CHRIST

rogance". The fear of the Lord is associated with avoiding evil - and it's avoiding evil by allowing ourselves to be guided by God's wise counsel. When we relate this to the local church context, we'd expect to see Christlikeness and the fruit of the Spirit as opposed to attitudes and lifestyles which conform to world trends. There'll be a deliberate avoidance of sin based on a shared understanding of the Bible's standards of purity and godliness. Holy living will also be humble living, with the proper level of subjection as the Bible directs. And all this in a loving atmosphere where real care is being expressed for each other.

Well, we've been exploring how the fear of the Lord was certainly known in the Jerusalem church, and reaching beyond the city itself. On one occasion which we can read about in Acts chapter 5, a husband and wife decided together to lie to the Holy Spirit. They were struck down dead by God in summary judgement, and, very understandably, we read on that: "great fear came upon all the church and upon all who heard these things ... and believers were increasingly added to the Lord, multitudes of both men and women" (Acts 5:11,14).

Once more, we come back to the text we're drawing these various features from - it's Acts 9:31 (NASB): "So the church throughout all Judea and Galilee and Samaria enjoyed peace, being built up; and, going on in the fear of the Lord and in the comfort of the Holy Spirit, it continued to increase."

We've previously dealt with it being edified or built up; with it going forward; with it experiencing the comfort of the Holy Spirit and what that meant; and we've just finished looking at what the fear of the Lord meant for it. Finally, then it only remains for us to examine the fact that it was increasing. For, you notice, we read, "... it continued to increase." In Jerusalem itself in those early days of Christianity, the number of Christians grew and grew. We read of a hundred and twenty (Acts 1:15), then three thousand more (2:41-42), then there's mention of at least five thousand (4:4), and then 'myriads' or multitudes (5:14) - as if they'd lost count of how many!

But let's not make the mistake of thinking that this increase is purely a numerical one. In Colossians chapter 1, verses 3 to 6, and describing the Gospel's ongoing work in us, we read one of Paul's prayers:

> "We always thank God, the Father of our Lord Jesus Christ, when we pray for you, since we heard of your faith in Christ Jesus and of the love that you have for all the saints, because of the hope laid up for you in heaven. Of this you have heard before in the word of the truth, the gospel, which has come to you, as indeed in the whole world it is bearing fruit and increasing—as it also does among you, since the day you heard it and understood the grace of God in truth ..."

That definitely deals with our spiritual growth, and that's something that certainly impacts on our ability to get on with one another, as the early Christians whom we've been thinking about, did. It's quite remarkable that the word 'church' is used in the singular in our Acts chapter nine text. It really confronts us with the reality of how unified these early Christians were. We know by this time there were in fact many churches

GET REAL ... LIVING EVERY DAY AS AN AUTHENTIC FOLLOWER OF CHRIST

throughout Judea (Galatians 1:22), not to mention Galilee and Samaria - and yet they're spoken of as one. At Jerusalem there were many companies forming in total one church in that city. And across the named provinces there were many other churches answering to that first one in Jerusalem, but such was the unity of their fellowship together, they could all be bracketed together in the singular here.

Remember, this was then the answer to the prayer of our Lord in John chapter 17, the most memorable feature of which was his request for unity among those who would believe through the witness the apostles were commissioned to give. In completing our brief sketch of life as it really ought to be in a local church, it would be good if we came back to the themes of John chapter 17, which actually are more than simply a single or repeated request for unity.

Jesus had said earlier in that John 17 prayer that he'd manifested his father's name. In other words, he lived out God's character from day to day (by his harmony with his Father, his joy, holiness, obedience and passion for souls). Later in his prayer, he asks that his followers might be kept loyal to that same manifestation.

Keep them in your name, he prays (vv.11,12). Then he unpacks this in five ways: first, that they may be one, even as there is unity within the Godhead. In other words, he requests that his disciples be united (v.11).

Second, he prayed: 'these things I speak in the world, that they may have my joy fulfilled in themselves' (v.13). That is, he asks that they be joyful.

Third, he prayed: 'I do not ask that you take them out of the world, but that you keep them from the evil one' (v.15). That was a prayer for them to be holy (as protected from evil and its source in Satan).

Fourth, he said: 'sanctify them in the truth; your word is truth' (v.17). In other words, his desire was that his followers should live in a way that was biblical. Fifth, the Lord prays: 'As you sent me into the world, so I have sent them into the world' (v.18). They were to show a passion for souls by being evangelical.

This is what the Lord prayed then, hours before he went to the cross. But, I think we can assume that this gives us an insight into his ongoing prayers for his disciples throughout this Church Age.

As his own life on earth displayed the name of his father in terms of the qualities of his life signifying what the character of his father is; so we're called upon to keep loyal to those same qualities – those of unity, joyfulness, holiness, being biblical and evangelical.

CHAPTER NINE: REALLY DEVOTED TO GOD'S SERVICE

Biblically, worship may be summed up in 2 words. The first main Bible word for worship is a word meaning 'submission'. In the (Greek) Old Testament it's found in Deuteronomy chapter 6 where we read how Moses told the Israelites: "You shall love the Lord your God with all your heart, with all your soul, and with all your might ... you yourself shall worship the Lord your God, and Him only you will serve" (Deuteronomy 6:5,13). In other words, truly loving the Lord demands all of our heart, all of our soul, and all of our strength. We cannot love the Lord in this way and still, at the same time, be devoted to, and chase after, the things of this world. These two loves are incompatible for the apostle John says: "If anyone loves the world, the love of the Father is not in him" (1 John 2:15).

Now, the verse we read from Deuteronomy chapter 6 a moment ago not only warned us against having divided affection and loyalties – but it then, you remember, went on to show us that wholehearted love for God precedes and underpins genuine worship of the true God: "love the Lord your God ... worship the Lord your God." Love and worship belong together – and this must surely also apply in the mistaken case of loving the world.

Let me explain. Through our own greed, lust and pride the world draws us away, and we end up compromising our affections. What's going on when that happens? The world system is demanding from us a competing submission and effort – one which is necessary if we're to obtain its desirable things like fame, success and financial rewards. Our affection and our allegiance to God become correspondingly diluted. And the resulting reality is that what we're devoted to - and what or whom we're submitted to, actually determines whom it is that we're worshipping (irrespective of any contrary claims we may make).

Let's try to make this even clearer. In Luke chapter 4, we find the Devil seeking worship. The scene is the three culminating temptations which he put to our Lord Jesus. In reply, Jesus used this same word for worship (the one with the idea of submission) when he answered the Devil's temptation by saying: "You shall worship [proskuneo] the Lord your God, and serve Him only." This was said immediately after the Devil had – quite literally – promised Jesus the world in exchange for Jesus being prepared to worship him and submit his allegiance to Satan.

We have to recognize this was a very specific temptation made in special circumstances. But, nonetheless, doesn't it seem to imply (consistent with what we've already seen based on Deuteronomy 6) that it's within Satan's domain to confer worldly honours (such as gain and glory), for which submission to his authority is his asking price? 'Worship' of the Devil, in this sense of submission, takes place whenever a person looks to the world system to satisfy his or her fleshly appetites because of the fact that "the whole world lies in the power of the evil one" (1 John 5:19). Worship is in reality a lifestyle choice.

The worship which the Devil is shown to seek after is achieved through our orientation to the world system. The choice that was presented to the Lord is, albeit in a far more general way, set before us by Paul in Romans 12, by James in James 4 and by John in 1 John 2. These texts warn us against conforming to, having friendship with, and loving the world. Isn't this the same basic issue? How far do conforming to, having friendship with and entertaining actual love for the world take us in the direction of giving the Devil what he's looking for? (After all, the Romans 12 reference has the context of worship).

Those who aspire to 'live the dream' down here by sacrificing time and effort to get ahead - to gain worldly things - scarcely realize that they've stepped into an alternative system of worship, irrespective of how orthodox their views are and however faithful their church attendance is.

Turning from Luke chapter 4 to John chapter 4, we find it's now the Father who's seeking worshippers. Those yielding to his will receive the privilege of accessing heaven from within a spiritual house on earth. The word for worship here in John chapter 4 is again the same worship word meaning submission – as when the Israelites in Egypt bowed in worship to God when they heard God was going to deliver them (Exodus 4:31); and it was used again during the dedication of Solomon's Temple—when the people saw the temple filled with the glory of the Lord and fell face down on the ground worshipping the Lord (2 Chronicles 7:3).

It seems clear that, when used to describe worship, this is a word which represents both the outward physical expression and the internal attitude of reverent submission on the part of the worshipper.

In Matthew 2:1-2, it's recorded that Magi came from the East to Jerusalem and said, "Where is the One who has been born King of the Jews? For we saw His star in the east, and came to worship Him." This same term 'worship' or 'submission' is again used in Matthew 2:11: "And having come into the house, the Magi found the child with Mary His mother, and having fallen down they worshipped Him." That is, they expressed their reverence and submission to the one born King of the Jews. There's a wonderful quote from William Temple which is spot on with our theme:

"Worship is the submission of all our nature to God. It is the quickening of conscience by His holiness; the nourishment of mind with His truth; the purifying of imagination by His Beauty; the opening of the heart to His love; the surrender of will to His purpose – and all of this gathered up in adoration, the most selfless emotion of which our nature is capable and therefore the chief remedy for that self-centeredness which is our original sin and the source of all actual sin."

Let's now take a look together at the second of the Bible's main worship words, which is a word meaning 'service' – 'latreuo'. In Exodus 20:5 (and in Deuteronomy 5:9), when the second of the famous Ten Commandments talks about neither worshipping nor 'serving' any graven image, it's this worship word that's used to express the Lord's command that Israel is to serve him without using graven images. On the brink of the Israelites finally setting foot in the Promised Land, they're told

(Deuteronomy 4:16, 19; 7:4, 16) not to 'serve' other gods, neither the gods of the peoples of the land and, indeed, nor are they to worship and serve the sun, moon, and stars. And after the Lord had brought them in and defeated all of their enemies, Joshua says (in Joshua 24:14) "Now, therefore, fear the LORD and serve Him in sincerity and truth; and put away the gods which your fathers served beyond the River and in Egypt; and serve the LORD".

Originally, this worship word which is often translated as 'serve' – as we've just read - was in fact a secular term meaning to work for hire or wages, but in the (Greek) Old Testament it's used to express either the worship of pagan gods or Israel's service of the true and living God. Right away, we're faced up with this basic fact that: who or what we serve is the actual object of our worship.

As we begin to dig even deeper into the meaning of worship in the form of service we now need to take a look at the noun form of this word in Romans 12:1-2 where Paul says:

> "I urge you, brethren, by the mercies of God, to present your bodies a living and holy sacrifice, acceptable to God, which is your spiritual service of worship. And do not be conformed to this world, but be transformed by the renewing of your mind, so that you may prove what the will of God is, that which is good and acceptable and perfect."

I'd go so far to say that there could be modern methods and styles of worship which would appear to be ruled out by this.

When he says: present your bodies a living sacrifice, holy, well-pleasing to God, which is (literally) your reasoning or reasonable service, Paul's telling us that worship definitely involves thinking through our response to God and, in fact, worship's in harmony with the very highest reason, and is far from an unthinking emotional response or mere ecstatic mood feeling.

This brings us on to another example of this worship word meaning 'service' as performed in a corporate way by God's Old Testament people, although the reference to it is in fact found in the New Testament, also in Romans, this time chapter 9, verse 4, where Paul refers to: "... my kinsmen ... whose is the service of God" (Romans 9:3,4). As we said, the reference is to Israel, but the very same word group translated here as 'service' (latreia) is used of God's New Testament people also worshipping corporately in Philippians 3:3 where Paul says we ... "worship in the Spirit of God and glory in Christ Jesus and put no confidence in the flesh".

The corporate worship of the people of God as expressed in this distinctive word is throughout all the Bible only ever directed to the God and Father of the Lord Jesus in the sense of "you shall ... serve Him only" (Luke 4:8). Now, this in no way detracts, of course, from the fact that the Lord Jesus is himself truly God nor from the fact that it was right for individuals who met him on earth to worship him.

But it shows how it's no mere protocol or habit that those in biblical Churches of God may very well address themselves to the One who is "the God and Father of our Lord Jesus" when coming together to worship God as they keep the Lord's com-

GET REAL ... LIVING EVERY DAY AS AN AUTHENTIC FOLLOWER OF CHRIST

mand to break bread each Sunday morning. Actually, this – linking back to our reading in Romans 9:4 and the 'service of God' – this goes right to the heart of a very important revelation regarding worship, which is that there's a type of worship that's corporately engaged in by the people of God – now equally as in Old Testament times by Israel.

This is worship that's distinct from the personal worship we can offer at all times; it's corporate worship, and may in fact only be offered to 'the Father', that is, neither to the Lord Jesus nor to 'our Father' – but specifically to the God and Father of our Lord Jesus. According to Hebrews 2:12, our Lord Jesus is himself a worshipper who leads the congregation singing praises! Basically, that's why New Testament Churches of God were - and are - in existence! It's because God the Father wants this highest form of corporate worship from his people now, just as he received worship from Israel in the past.

CHAPTER TEN: REALLY WORSHIPPING IN SPIRIT AND TRUTH

Christ's death totally reformed the way in which God's gathered people come before God in worship. The cross is explained in both the Bible letter to the Romans and the Hebrews, but these letters present it in two very different contexts. In Romans, we're invited to picture the scene presented as that of an individual before the bar in God's judgement hall. By contrast, the scene that presents itself in Hebrews is that of a worshiping people before the throne in God's heavenly sanctuary. We'll totally miss the point of these letters if we fail to notice that. And, another thing, when we come to the Hebrews' letter, which is going to be our main focus, we need to identify very clearly those who are being addressed. This is a letter written in corporate terms rather than dealing with the case of an individual, and the current standing of those addressed is comparable with that of the nation of Israel in the past.

Another distinction worth making is to observe that the letter to the Ephesians relates to the standing of members of the Church which is Christ's Body (Ephesians 1:22-23). It explores 'the heavenlies.' Hebrews, on the other hand, focuses on the privileges of disciples worshiping together in the New Testament community of the churches of God (1 Corinthians 11:16). It explores 'the Holies.' Hebrews is THE book which presents Christ as our high priest (a 'forgotten letter'?). This is the high table-land of Scripture as the Holy Spirit expounds for us the significance of all the detail which God was so particular about in the time of Moses.

And within the letter to the Hebrews, chapters 8-10 give us the Spirit's typical teaching, disclosing the new way of corporate worship. At Hebrews 8:1,2 we reach the summit of the preceding discussion: "We have such a High Priest ... a minister of the sanctuary [holies]." It's here we discover that Christ's ministry is in 'the holies' (Hebrews 8:2). We need to pause and unpack that term. This is the first occurrence of 'hagia' (a neuter plural adjective). Curiously, there's no actual noun (e.g. 'place') being qualified – and that ought to get our attention – for this is a feature that's unique to Hebrews.

'The way of the holies' (9:8, την των αγιων οδον) is used in a dual sense. ('Holies' occurs in 8:2; 9:1, 2, 3, 8, 12). Israel's high priest annually entered into the holies' (εις τα αγια) on earth typifying the Holies in heaven (24, 25; 10:19). This word is found ten times in this section, once later in Hebrews, but nowhere else. This wonderful section of 3 chapters is not only marked out by its 10 mentions of 'hagia,' but there's something else. There are six occurrences of a specific word for worship ('latreia' and 'latreuo'). in this section, and these are its first mentions in the letter to the Hebrews, with few beyond this section. This sudden repetition comes in this section which is defined by its repeated mention of 'the Holies.' It implies that the purpose of God's people entering the Holies is for divine worship in the highest sense possible. Biblically, as we've seen, worship is explained as submission and service. This further strengthens the case that those being addressed in this Hebrews letter are God's gathered people who submit to the God of Scripture and serve and worship according to his Word.

In the Old Testament, God gave instructions for the heavenly sanctuary to be copied within the earthly tabernacle. Moses was told: "See that you make it according to the pattern shown you in the mount" (Hebrews 8:5; Exodus 25:9,40). It was submission to God and serving by a pattern that expressed the highest form of worship known to us, a type only ever spoken of as being presented to the Father (e.g. Romans 9:4). At the centre of the nation's worship stood the Tabernacle. To this sanctuary, God's people then brought their specified offerings, to the altar in the courtyard that surrounded the special tent known as the Tabernacle. This is what the approach to God by his people in worship looked like back then.

Bear with me, if you will, for we'll be richly rewarded if we can get into just a little more detail – detail which is explicitly there in Hebrews. There were two compartments in the 'copy' made by Moses - an outer, sometimes known as 'the first tabernacle', called the Holy place; and an inner, sometimes known as 'the second tabernacle,' called 'the Holy of holies.' And these two sections were separated by a veil which acted as the dividing line between them inside the overall tent of the Tabernacle. Chapter nine and verse eight says: "The Holy Spirit is signifying this, that the way into the holy place has not yet been disclosed while the outer tabernacle is yet standing" (Hebrews 9:8).

In Hebrews 9:2,6 some Bible versions use the more confusing term of 'the first tabernacle' (RV; KJV), but as mentioned,

GET REAL ... LIVING EVERY DAY AS AN AUTHENTIC FOLLOWER OF CHRIST 75

this clearly refers to the outer compartment. If a term is used 3 times close together, we may assume it always has the same meaning (so also in v.8). Let's come back to verse 8 again. "The Holy Spirit is signifying this, that the way into the holy place has not yet been disclosed while the outer tabernacle is yet standing" (Hebrews 9:8). This is first of all making a very straightforward, historical, factual statement – the Israelites were prevented from seeing their high priest going through the veil that divided the two sections by virtue of the fact that the outer section also had sides consisting of frames with curtains and coverings draped over it. These were obviously not transparent, so people couldn't see inside.

To have removed that outer section would literally have exposed the passage of the high priest to all as he made his way annually into the inner section. But there's something more than a straightforward, factual, historical statement here, for the Holy Spirit, treating this as one of the major types of Scripture, is signifying that the removal of what the first or outer section represents, portrays for us the disclosure of our present opportunity for the spiritual worship of God's people taking place in the true holies which is located in heaven – the very one of which, you remember, this structure built by Moses was a mere copy.

Let the Bible text further clarify that what we're saying is true. The significant point being that the outer tabernacle (alone) symbolized the (entire) past way of approach - which was removed when Christ came. It's verse 9 that tells us that the outer section of the Tabernacle was a symbol for the time of the Old Testament, referred to in some Bible versions as 'the present time.' That's capable of being misunderstood, and we need to be clear it's not meaning 'the time now present' (as per the RV), but rather 'the time then present' (as in the KJV). To sum up, the outer tabernacle section symbolized the past way of approach to God by a worshiping people. What's called 'the present time' (of v.9) ended with the 'time of reformation' (of v.10), that is, the time of Christ's First Advent, when he was shown to be the true Veil – giving full access to God in worship by his people.

Jesus came to take away 'the first' so as to set 'the second' before others. He said, "BEHOLD, I HAVE COME TO DO YOUR WILL." He takes away the first in order to establish the second, we're told in Hebrews 10:9. This is equivalent in meaning to the taking away of the first or outer tabernacle section, so that he might 'set before others' ('establish') the second - with 'the second' being the manner in which God has willed his New Testament people's approach to the Holies in heaven. As long as the first (outer) tabernacle blocked the view into the second (inner) tabernacle, the way into the copy wasn't disclosed (literally), and as long as the old order of approach involving animals remained in force, the new order and way into the reality in heaven wasn't disclosed either. (I'm not saying 'the first' in chapters 9 & 10 directly refers to the same things - but indirectly they do, in terms of what they represented).

Let's come to the amazing words of Hebrews chapter 10, verse 19: "since we have confidence to enter the holy place by the blood of Jesus." Commentators generally widen the applicability of this statement as applying to 'all access to God through the sacrifice of Christ.' This disregards the clues that are to be found in its context. Take the first verse of the chapter, 'For the Law ... can never, by the same sacrifices which they offer continually year by year, make perfect those who draw near' (Hebrews 10:1).

And then, on the other side of verse 19, we have the command: "Let us draw near ..." (Hebrews 10:22). That's drawing near in the same way, that is, as a gathered people and at set times and in corporate worship. In keeping with the general theme of the letter, the "drawing near" in the passage under review has a more specific reference.

The fact is that in both Testaments God's gathered people were required to gather for worship at stated times in a prescribed way. You'll recall we began by making the point that those addressed in Hebrews are viewed as being in the same circumstances as Old Testament Israel. Back then it was a case of "Three times in a year all your males shall appear before the LORD your God in the place which He chooses" (Deuteronomy 16:16). It referred to when God's people gathered in their holy convocations at the set feasts. Compare that with the situation in the New Testament. The Lord had said: "This do ... in remembrance of Me" (1 Corinthians 11:23-25). And this ordinance was to be observed when local churches of God gather (1 Corinthians 11:18) on the first day of every week (Acts 20:7; 1 Corinthians 16:2).

In both Old and New Testaments, we find a gathered people at set times for corporate worship. The difference is that in worship that's now in spirit and truth (John 4:24), 'the way of the holies' (Hebrews 9:8) is now the 'new and living way' (Hebrews 10:20) by which God's New Covenant people draw near to worship in the sanctuary in the heavens. When our High Priest "through His own blood, entered in once for all into the holies" (Hebrews 9:12), he initiated the new way of approach for God's people. We're invited to draw near in worship now (Hebrews 10:19) to that same heavenly sanctuary into which our high priest, Jesus, entered in resurrection as our forerunner (Hebrews 6:19,20).

CHAPTER ELEVEN: REALLY DEALING WITH DISILLUSIONMENT

No treatment of the reality of Christian living and service could surely be considered complete if we didn't cover the issue of disillusionment. It's not that we could ever, rightly, be disappointed with God, nor in his instruction for our lives. But we can so easily become disillusioned by what we perceive as the behaviour of others, as well as disappointed in our own performance.

The Apostle Paul recognized, and spoke to, the very real danger of losing heart (2 Corinthians 4). But first, the words of Bible preacher James Stewart, from his book 'Heralds of God', have remained with me, no doubt because I sense a reality in them. He wrote: 'Surely there are few figures so pitiable as the disillusioned minister of the Gospel. High hopes cheered him on his way, but now the indifference ... of the world, the lack of ... visible results, the discovery of appalling pettiness ... the feeling of personal futility, all these have seared his soul. No longer does the zeal of God's house devour him. No longer does he mount the pulpit steps in thrilled expectancy that Jesus Christ will come amongst his folk that day travelling in the greatness of his strength, mighty to save ... The man has lost heart.'

A Christian with any years of experience would, I suggest, be in denial to dispute the reality that Stewart describes. The Apostle Paul experienced it too, amid the brutal opposition he often had to endure, and the defection of those who'd once been converted and had been loyal supporters. So much so, that when he takes up his 'pen,' as it were, and writes the chapter we know as Second Corinthians chapter 4. It seems to come across very clearly that his thrust is on how to avoid losing heart. It would seem that he overcame this tendency by doing three things. Three things that commend themselves to us, for us to emulate. And they are: first, remembering how we ourselves once received mercy; second, striving for transparency in plainly manifesting the truth; third, habitually making it our aim to exhibit what he calls 'the dying of Jesus' in a disciplined lifestyle.

Let's try to unpack them briefly, in turn. Paul continually remembered that he was a vessel of God's undeserved mercy. 2 Corinthians 4:1 literally says, "as we have been mercied (once for all), we do not lose heart." The mercy Paul had received from and found in Christ protected his mind and heart from temptations. We need to keep on remembering what we were before mercy came to us. We have to count God's mercy in Christ as the greatest joy of our life when surrounded by any measure of rejection and opposition. When we tend to get exasperated by the failures we think we see so readily in others, it's a sobering corrective to return in thought to the extent to which we ourselves benefit from God's mercy, that is, his withholding of what we truly deserved.

Then, as any reading of the New Testament narrative would support, Paul always preached, with a transparent integrity. He announced the plain Word of God. Paul refused to walk in craftiness and scheming to gain a following. He refused to adulterate, or in any way to handle deceitfully, the plain manifestation of the Word of God. He didn't resort to whatever things were available in the Corinthian culture to enhance the message or method. He didn't use the driving music and mass hysteria of the Aphrodite worship. He didn't use the glamour and hype of the Isthmus games in Corinth to excite awareness and credibility. He didn't promise prosperity in the robust Corinthian economy. He didn't enlist Greek drama or the sophists' rhetorical form as a means of mass appeal. He simply preached gospel truth to men's consciences in the sight of God - no matter how negative the response he received. It may be discouraging to think that we preach to those who are blinded by their own sinful ignorance and by Satan's power. But if we accept that truth, we'll not expect from other things what only God can do in their heart.

Finally, Paul practised self-denial. 'The dying of Jesus' was his adopted worldview. He was so overwhelmed at the self-denial of God the Son for a sinner like himself that it transformed his thinking towards others at all times, infusing it with reality. In such an attitude, there's no room for self-importance, jealousy of another's easier circumstances, or for wallowing in self-pity. There's only room for the self-denying joy of seeing the grace of God spread to more people. Self-denial on earth is fuelled not by what we see with our eyes now, but what we see in the future. We may see sermons going unheeded, loving rebukes rewarded with hatred, sincerity rewarded with deception, loyalty returned with betrayal. Only the future seen by faith can cause the trials of a self-denying ministry to be called 'momentary, light affliction.'

What's more, I think we should surface some realistic concerns relating to those deeply committed to the Christian faith and serving God's purpose in their lives. There's the real danger of emotional depletion. Many in positions of Christian responsibility run on empty emotional tanks, brought about by continual output in terms of teaching and leadership; always being 'on display' as a public figure; facing criticism of their ministry; and the pressure of relentless expectations. Those with a shepherd's heart discover sheep are messy creatures. Burnout can result from the defections of those on whom a lot of effort had been expended.

Then there's the lack of setting of appropriate boundaries in their working arrangements. If, when emotionally depleted or hurting, we don't find something God-honouring to fill our emotional tanks with, we'll be vulnerable to something that isn't. Do we build fences around our thought life in relation to, for example, such things as we view online?

And there's also spiritual deception. Because of constantly doing things, it's easy to confuse doing them with actually being spiritual. For example, being constantly in the Bible in order to prepare a talk. It's easy to confuse this with reading the Bible devotionally. Leading public praying too can fool someone into thinking they're leading a life of personal prayer. And responsible persons are often put on some kind of spiritual pedestal. All too easily, the estimation others have about their spiritual life (however unrealistic) can become their own.

And now, a word, if I may, to those who may have been specifically called to pastoral or leadership duties. When Microsoft's then CEO, Steve Ballmer, retired, there were those who felt that the company had failed to react to the trend to take PCs away from desks. Some went further and said they'd missed the key new concepts of search, mobile and cloud. We can all too easily fall into the kind of mentality that wants to hold on to what we have, what has performed well for us in the past, and so prefer not to try to come to terms with new ideas. In spiritual terms, there are key new ideas we need to get up to speed with, including the trends of our society towards rapidly increasing secularization; the pluralization of religious belief; and the privatization of faith. If it's true that there was a time when Microsoft confused programs and products with their basic reason for existing in business, we need to make sure our focus is not on Gospel Meetings of the type belonging to a past era, but on evangelism per se; and perhaps also not to overly rely on meetings to do the work of mentoring. What else might we be failing to react to on our watch?

Change can be overwhelming, and modern lifestyles throw up challenges that can seem unsurmountable. It's easy to become overtaken with a feeling that we're being stretched beyond our capacity to handle it. I think the best thing we can do is to rewind back to the absolute Bible basics of our pastoral responsibility. What must underpin our work is a real sense that we were called by God to what we do, otherwise we'd quickly give up. And we were called to a dual commitment. First, a commitment to the Word of God (1 Thessalonians 2:4,9). This aspect of our calling as shepherds is to act as stewards and heralds of God's Word, both guarding it and enthusing over it. Then there's to be our commitment to the People of God (1 Thessalonians 2:7,11) - acting as a mother and father in terms of caring gently and educating diligently.

The final chapter of the letter to the Hebrews, gives an appealing glimpse of the character of anyone in a Christian leadership role. A person like that is to be memorable (Hebrews 13:7); to be persuasive through earning respect (Hebrews 13:17); and to be approachable by being appropriately vulnerable (among as well as over; Hebrews 13:24).

And to give some clarity as to the caring role to be exercised, where better to turn to than the great shepherd Psalm, the much-loved 23rd. From its verses, we can explore four freedoms; it was always the duty of the shepherd to provide freedom in four areas. Verse 2 says, 'he makes me lie down in green pastures.' In other words, the shepherd's first duty is to ensure freedom from hunger. Pastoral care for the spiritual flock demands it be fed from God's Word. I remember hearing about a group of Christian leaders pausing for a lunch stop while on a journey. They approached a restaurant only to read the notice on the door: 'closed for lunch.' They smiled to themselves that this should never be said of them. The teaching pastor is to be ready to share God's Word at any time (2 Timothy 4:2).

Psalm 23 next presents us with the imagery of dark valleys, where the presence of the shepherd close by was to be the essential feature. This likely has in view the moving of the flock up the hillside valley routes to the higher summer pastures, as suggested by Philip Keller. The valleys etched into the hillsides not only provided access, but in these fertile channels, typical predators had also made their homes. God's flock, in the same way, needs to be free of fear, particularly from the prowling lion looking to devour from its number. That's the graphic way the Apostle Peter describes the Devil and his tactics (1 Peter 5:8). In Acts 20, while talking to Ephesian elders, the Apostle Paul's expressed fear, on behalf of the flock, was in relation to those who infiltrated the community in some sense in order to press their own agendas.

The same fourth verse brings up mention of the shepherd's equipment – his rod and staff. These allowed him to both protect and guide his sheep. There's talk of comfort here, and so we relate this to a freedom from tensions. These can all too easily enter into church life. The rod was to deter wild animals, so perhaps the main source of tension we can relate to this would come from outside the local church in terms of opposition, even persecution, but more generally simply the result of living in an environment that's increasingly hostile to the Christian faith and its distinctive values.

Finally, there's freedom from aggravations. This is suggested by the reference in verse five to the anointing oil. This is what middle Eastern shepherds apparently used (see Philip Keller's book on this Psalm, "A Shepherd Looks at Psalm 23", written by a shepherd) to rub into areas such as around the nose of a sheep. The aim was to stop flies laying eggs, and in turn to prevent this leading to any infection of the exposed flesh. Strained relationships tending to divisiveness needs courageous and skilful handling. How vital an area of watchfulness this is! Very easily, inter-personal aggravations can spill over as petty jealousies creep in.

Sometimes those concerned fail to treat these things by applying the procedure the Lord himself outlined in Matthew's gospel chapter 18. He'd also been talking about sheep, including one in danger of being lost to the flock. If someone has been sinned against, s/he's to take a couple of witnesses, and interact directly and discreetly with only the person who's implicated in this matter. It should only escalate to an issue involving the church leadership team if resistance is encountered, and that's potentially more serious than the initial fault in question, because it becomes aggravated at that point. Oh, to be free not only of aggravations, but of tensions, fear and hunger!

CHAPTER TWELVE: REALLY LIVING ABOVE MEDIOCRITY

Paul wrote to Timothy: "Kindle afresh the gift of God which is in you through the laying on of my hands" (2 Timothy 1:6).

And Amy Carmichael wrote:

> "O for a passionate passion for souls,
>
> O for a pity that yearns!
>
> O for the love that loves unto death,
>
> O for the fire that burns!"

These quotes set the scene for us. They invoke the imagery of someone 'on fire for God.' That's always a remarkable sight, no less so than the burning bush that grabbed Moses' attention. It wasn't so much the burning that was extraordinary there, but the fact that it kept on burning. There was no 'burnout' because God was in it. God is a consuming fire, but by his mercies, we are not consumed.

But there will be times when this world's 'chill factor' will lower our spiritual temperature. It would appear that this was the case with Timothy – at very least something had changed and he was less enthused about the things of God. It's good when God draws our attention to this kind of coolness, and draws us back to himself in what we can rightly call 'revival.'

Jim Packer, in his book Keep in Step with the Spirit (p.245), tries to picture what revival looks like, based on biblical examples among the kings of Judah and the later Jewish exiles who returned from captivity in foreign lands to rebuild their life of national service for God in Jerusalem. He draws the complete picture with four brush strokes. These are: God coming down; God's Word coming home; God's purity coming through; and finally, God's people coming alive. I would like to borrow the headings, which seem an excellent starting point, and we'll try to develop each of them briefly.

First, God comes down. Nowhere is this better captured than in the prophet Isaiah's prayer request:

> "Oh, that You would rend the heavens and come down, that the mountains might quake at Your presence – as fire kindles the brushwood, as fire causes water to boil – to make Your name known to Your adversaries, that the nations may tremble at Your presence!" (Isaiah 64:1).

Revival brings a greater sense of God. And what's pictured here is an awesome sense of his majesty, made known through the nearness of his power. At times, we can become lacklustre in our spiritual lives. It's as if we are like someone treading water, but going nowhere. Things settle into a dull routine. We relax about the things of God – and even rationalize a leisurely approach to prayer and praise.

GET REAL ... LIVING EVERY DAY AS AN AUTHENTIC FOLLOWER OF CHRIST

It's when God stirs us to cry out like Isaiah with the same great depth of feeling that communicates itself to us through the passion of the language used: 'Oh, that You would rend the heavens and come down, that the mountains might quake at Your presence – as fire kindles the brushwood, as fire causes water to boil – to make Your name known to Your adversaries, that the nations may tremble at Your presence!' Can we relate to times when we've feelings like that? We're very conscious of our inconsistencies, but we want God to have more of us, and move us from our state of lethargy to higher ground.

I'm writing this in The Philippines, and up in a remote mountain village where there's now a church of God, the young women sang sweetly the words of the old hymn: 'Lord ... plant my feet on higher ground ... on heaven's tableland ...' Amy Carmichael, whom we heard from earlier, has another poem called 'God's Mountaineer,' I think, and the thrust of it is that we should all aspire to leave the lowlands of mediocrity behind us in the passionate pursuit of a greater sense of God.

Until now, we've used Old Testament examples, and it's true that in the Church Age, the Holy Spirit resides in each and every true believer in the Lord Jesus, but there's the danger of him being quenched, and even entire church services can become perfunctory. Something of the Old Testament sense is perhaps described in Paul's letter to Corinth about a church service ...

> "If, therefore, the whole church comes together and ... all prophesy, and an unbeliever or outsider enters, he is convicted by all, he is called to account by all,

the secrets of his heart are disclosed, and so, falling on his face, he will worship God and declare that God is really among you" (1 Corinthians 14:23-25 ESV).

Of course, there's also the case of the church at Laodicea in Revelation chapter 3, where their love had become lukewarm, and lacking the sense of the immediacy of God we've just read about. The hymn-writer captures what's desired in the words: 'and all assembled caused to feel the presence of our God.'

But that's only one brush stroke in this biblical painting of Revival. Three to go, we must move on to the second, which we said was when God's Word comes home. Staying with the prophet Isaiah, he also wrote: "But this is the one to whom I will look: he who is humble and contrite in spirit and trembles at my word" (Isaiah 66:2; and check out the trembling in Ezra 9). There's an impressive chapter in the book of Nehemiah. It's the eighth, and describes the people all gathered as one before one of Jerusalem's gates to listen to God's Word being taught. In a real sense, this was the first time Bible exposition was done as it is today, for there those people heard the Bible read in what was no longer their mother tongue.

While away in exile for 70 years, they'd lost their old language, at least for the most part. The Bible teachers that day had to explain its terms more carefully than ever before. We're told the Levites "read from the book, from the law of God, translating to give the sense so that they understood the reading" (v.8). But notice the next verse: "the people were weeping when they heard the words of the law." And later it says: "the people went away to ... celebrate because they understood the words which had been made known to them" (v.12). The report of that emotional day goes on to describe how they not only gained new insights, but they took immediate action to rectify past omission, putting what they'd heard into practice. This is the second feature of true revival. It's when people feel the impact of the Bible's authority. A sharp contrast over against the silencing of its implications within the secular worldview.

If that's the second brush stroke, now we come to the third. After God coming down and revealing something of his majesty, we then had God's Word coming home to our hearts. Next in sequence, is when God's purity comes through, as it certainly did to Isaiah when God spoke to him in a vision:

> "In the year that King Uzziah died I saw the Lord sitting upon a throne, high and lifted up; and the train of his robe filled the temple. Above him stood the seraphim. Each had six wings: with two he covered his face, and with two he covered his feet, and with two he flew. And one called to another and said: "Holy, holy, holy is the Lord of hosts; the whole earth is full of his glory!" And the foundations of the thresholds shook at the voice of him who called, and the house was filled with smoke. And I said: "Woe is me! For I am lost; for I am a man of unclean lips, and I dwell in the midst of a people of unclean lips; for my eyes have seen the King, the Lord of hosts!"

> Then one of the seraphim flew to me, having in his hand a burning coal that he had taken with tongs from the altar. And he touched my mouth and said: "Behold, this has touched your lips; your guilt is taken away, and your sin atoned for." And I heard the voice of the Lord saying, "Whom shall I send, and who will go for us?" Then I said, "Here I am! Send me." And he said, "Go, and say to this people ..." (Isaiah 6:1-8 ESV).

Isaiah wasn't at the beginning of his prophetic ministry at this point in his life. He'd served God during the reign of the now deceased king (Isaiah 1:1). But this was a step-change for him. God had drawn close in a special way, and spoken to him personally. And the most dramatic effect was to bring about a conviction of sin, and an abhorrence of the guilt and ugliness of sin. Even among experienced Christians, God's holiness can become eclipsed by the narcissism of a self-absorbed form of evangelicalism.

Finally, after God comes down (or makes us more acutely aware of his presence within this Church Age), and his Word comes home to our hearts, and as a result his purity comes through to us, as with Isaiah, it's then that God's People come alive. They come alive with a holy boldness to intercede, to witness, to worship. This can be in stark contrast to the slumber of some who remain faithful to Victorian forms without the freshness of an up-to-date experience of God.

There's an interesting thing recorded of David, the king, in Psalm 78:65: "Then the LORD awoke as if from sleep." What

GET REAL ... LIVING EVERY DAY AS AN AUTHENTIC FOLLOWER OF CHRIST

does this mean? Does God really fall asleep? Well no, this is poetry. Psalm 78 is a long psalm which traces the history of God's people Israel in Old Testament times. It traces the ebb and flow of their spiritual condition throughout the period when the land was ruled by judges, down to the time of Samuel. Even in his days, a man who'd great influence with God through his godly praying – even in his time - a disaster happened to the people and the Ark of the Covenant which symbolised God's presence among his people. It was captured by the enemy. God said it was as if his glory had left them. Things were at a very low ebb indeed. 'Then the LORD awoke from sleep.'

This was the awakening in David's heart as God raised him up to play a role in bringing in better times for his people. It wasn't permanent however, and God would later, again through the prophet Isaiah, describe dark times that his people would pass through, as the call came to them to "Arise, shine, ... The glory of the LORD has risen upon you."

When our lives too are dull and sleepy, and we're in danger of losing a clear sense of the reality of it all, then we, too, need to draw near to God such that he draws near to us (James 4:8). The way we do that is by engaging seriously with his Word, turning what we read into prayer. This will inevitably lead to us purifying our hearts as we humble ourselves in God's presence (James 4:8-10). It's this that then energises our on-going service for God, making us to be "fervent in spirit, serving the Lord" (Romans 12:11).

I pray these thoughts will be used by God to stir us to get real, for the thing the Lord spoke against so often when he walked this planet was the empty pretence, the hypocrisy of the lives of people around him.

Did you love *Get Real ... Living Every Day as an Authentic Follower of Christ*? Then you should read *Deepening Our Relationship With Christ* by Brian Johnston!

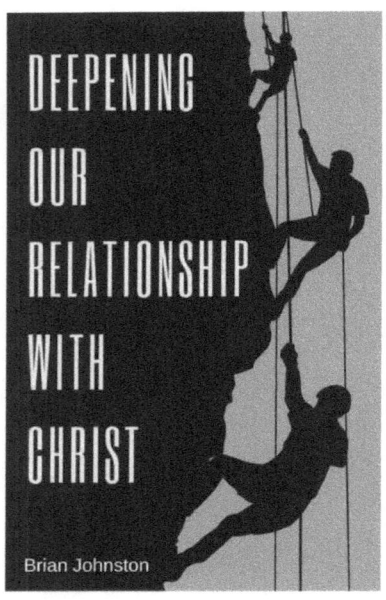

The first step in our relationship with Jesus is accepting Him as our Saviour - but that's just the beginning! In this short book, Brian Johnston expounds 8 important ways that every Christian should deepen their personal relationship with Christ.

1. In being in union with Him
2. In being built on Him
3. In being United by and with Him
4. In following Him
5. In owning Him as Head of the Body
6. In being added alongside Him

7. In being subject to Him as Son over God's House
8. In remembering Him

Also by Brian Johnston

Healthy Churches - God's Bible Blueprint For Growth
Hope for Humanity: God's Fix for a Broken World
First Corinthians: Nothing But Christ Crucified
Bible Answers to Listeners' Questions
Living in God's House: His Design in Action
Christianity 101: Seven Bible Basics
Nights of Old: Bible Stories of God at Work
Daniel Decoded: Deciphering Bible Prophecy
A Test of Commitment: 15 Challenges to Stimulate Your Devotion to Christ
John's Epistles - Certainty in the Face of Change
If Atheism Is True...
8 Amazing Privileges of God's People: A Bible Study of Romans 9:4-5
Learning from Bible Grandparents
Increasing Your Christian Footprint
Christ-centred Faith
Mindfulness That Jesus Endorses
Amazing Grace! Paul's Gospel Message to the Galatians
Abraham: Friend of God
The Future in Bible Prophecy
Unlocking Hebrews
Learning How To Pray - From the Lord's Prayer

About the Bush: The Five Excuses of Moses
Deepening Our Relationship With Christ
Really Good News For Today!
A Legacy of Kings - Israel's Chequered History
Minor Prophets: Major Issues!
The Tabernacle - God's House of Shadows
Tribes and Tribulations - Israel's Predicted Personalities
Once Saved, Always Saved - The Reality of Eternal Security
After God's Own Heart : The Life of David
Jesus: What Does the Bible Really Say?
God: His Glory, His Building, His Son
God's Appointment Calendar: The Feasts of Jehovah
Praying with Paul
Get Real ... Living Every Day as an Authentic Follower of Christ

About the Author

Born and educated in Scotland, Brian worked as a government scientist until God called him into full-time Christian ministry on behalf of the Churches of God (www.churchesofgod.info). His voice has been heard on Search For Truth radio broadcasts for over 30 years (visit www.searchfortruth.podbean.com) during which time he has been an itinerant Bible teacher throughout the UK and Canada. His evangelical and missionary work outside the UK is primarily in Belgium and The Philippines. He is married to Rosemary, with a son and daughter.

About the Publisher

Hayes Press (www.hayespress.org) is a registered charity in the United Kingdom, whose primary mission is to disseminate the Word of God, mainly through literature. It is one of the largest distributors of gospel tracts and leaflets in the United Kingdom, with over 100 titles and hundreds of thousands despatched annually.

Hayes Press also publishes Plus Eagles Wings, a fun and educational Bible magazine for children, and Golden Bells, a popular daily Bible reading calendar in wall or desk formats.

Also available are over 100 Bibles in many different versions, shapes and sizes, Christmas cards, Christian jewellery, Eikos Bible Art, Bible text posters and much more!

www.ingramcontent.com/pod-product-compliance
Lightning Source LLC
Chambersburg PA
CBHW071308040426
42444CB00009B/1926